The State in the Third Millennium

The State
in the
Third Millennium

Hans-Adam II
The Reigning Prince of Liechtenstein

van Eck Publishers

Bibliographic information published by the Deutsche Nationalbibliothek
The Deutsche Nationalbibliothek lists this publication in the Deutsche Nationalbibliografie; detailed bibliographic data are available in the Internet at http://dnb.d-nb.de.

1st Edition
Copyright © Prince Hans-Adam II of Liechtenstein 2009
www.vaneckverlag.li
Copy-editing by Katy Carter
Index by ISB&Index
Book design by Herbert Hofer
Printed in Liechtenstein by BVD Druck + Verlag AG, Schaan
ISBN: 978-3-905881-04-2

TABLE OF CONTENTS

Introduction	1
1. The right to self-determination—a personal conviction	5
2. The origins of the state	17
3. The role of religion in the formation of the state	21
4. The size of states and the influence of military technology	31
5. Monarchy, oligarchy, democracy	45
6. The American Revolution and indirect democracy	59
7. The Swiss constitution of 1848 and the path to direct democracy	63
8. Liechtenstein's constitutional reform of 2003	69
9. The deficiencies of traditional democracy	77
10. The state of the future	85
10.1 The constitutional state	91
10.2 The welfare state	107
10.3 The education system	117

10.4 Transportation	121
10.5 Public finances	127
10.6 The national currency	135
10.7 Other state duties	147
11 A constitution for the state of the future	151
12. Strategies to achieve the state of the future	157
13. A perspective on the third millennium	177
Appendix: A draft constitution for the state in the third millennium	183
Index	203

Introduction

First of all, I should like to thank everyone who has taken the trouble to read my manuscript and to whom I owe so many corrections, additions, and suggestions. This book is the result of a long and critical examination of the meaning and purpose of the state. I started this process as a high school student, as I mention in Chapter 1, and today, after my withdrawal from active politics, it still remains unfinished.

A friend of mine, a professor of constitutional philosophy with whom I often discussed my manuscript, asked me what type of a book this is supposed to be. Is it, he asked, a treatise on constitutional philosophy, a political manifesto, a memoir, or a history book? The more I think about it, the more it seems simply to be a cookbook of political recipes, gathered over centuries by my ancestors and over decades by myself. My hope is that these recipes will help to build a state for the third millennium, a state that can be enjoyed by as many people as possible. Whatever these political recipes may look like, one thing is certain: much can be learned from the political recipes of earlier centuries and millennia, but more modern recipes will be necessary to fulfill the wishes and needs of humanity in the third millennium. For part of the world population, the age of democracy started only at the end of the second millennium. It is to be hoped that democracy will shape the third millennium and the future of human history and not remain, as in earlier millennia, an event restricted in time and geography or, in other words, a footnote of history.

What kind of state does humanity want in the third millennium? President Kennedy, whom I had the honor to meet personally when I was a young man, said in his Inaugural Address in 1961: "Ask not what your country can do for you—ask what you can do for your country." As a young, idealistic person, I was in those days convinced by this statement. Today, I may not have lost all of my ideals, but decades of experience in national and international politics, including many years as the head of state of a small but modern democracy, have convinced me of the truth of the reverse statement: *Ask not what a citizen can do for the state, but rather what the state can do better for the citizen than any other organization.* This organization could be a community, an international organization, or a private company. I would like to set out in this book the reasons why the traditional state as a monopoly enterprise not only is an inefficient enterprise with a poor price–performance ratio, but even more importantly, becomes more of a danger for humanity the longer it lasts.

A critical approach to human history, especially of the 20th century, reveals the state as a real threat to the life and freedom of the individual. With this in mind, it is easy to understand those who disavow every form of governmental order. Does humanity wish to have a state in the third millennium? Is it not possible to realize finally the old utopia of a society without a state? The rejection of every form of government is widely known by the Greek term *anarchia* (anarchy), which was originally a peaceful movement based on private ownership. What anarchists probably have not sufficiently considered is that private ownership requires the rule of law. Without a state, the rule of law, which should include everybody, is very difficult to realize and hardly possible to maintain over a long period of time.

At the end of the 19th century, some anarchists came under the influence of socialist-communist ideology, which rejected private ownership and advocated violence. The goal of communism was a classless society without a state. During a transitional stage, this goal was to be attained through the dictatorship of the proletariat. The result was a totalitarian state, in whose concentration camps many more people were murdered than in the better known concentration camps of the Nazis. It is estimated that in the Soviet Union alone up to 20 million people were murdered for political reasons, and that the numbers in China may have been even higher. The experiment in Cambodia with so-called stone-age communism is supposed to have cost a third of the population their lives. Even if these figures are overestimations, they certainly exceed the estimated six million victims of National Socialism's concentration camps.

One can argue that there was at least a theoretical difference between National Socialism and communism. Whoever was born as a Jew remained a Jew and was killed by the Nazis in a concentration camp. Whoever was born as a class enemy had at least the theoretical possibility of converting to socialism and communism. Socialism and communism are therefore ideologically nearer to the world religions than National Socialism, but in political reality the difference was small. Those who were born class enemies were offered the chance of conversion only on rare occasions. But even the conversion to socialism and communism offered no protection against death in a concentration camp under Stalin, Mao Zedong, Pol Pot, and other dictators.

It would be a major success if in the third millennium, as described in this book, humanity were able to transform all states into service companies that worked for the people on the basis of direct and indirect democracy and the right of self-determination at the local level. Shareholders in this service company "state" would be its citizens, to whom the state would pay out profits in one way or the other as described in Chapter 10. However, as in mountain climbing, in politics it is wisest to take one step at a time. If you run, you may fall. For some, the steps in this book will appear too large; for others, too small. Yet perhaps in the fourth millennium, humanity may be able to ask the question: "Why do we need a state at all?"

Naturally, an anarchist could claim that a monarch from a family that has reigned for centuries cannot possibly be in favor of abolishing the state. In response, I should like to note that the Princes of Liechtenstein are not paid for their duties as head of state by either the state or the taxpayer. The total cost of our monarchy, in contrast to almost all other monarchies, is covered by the Prince's or the Princely House's private funds. It is true that being head of state offers many gratifying moments and certain advantages; but it is surely more of a hindrance than a necessity for happiness, not least because of the responsibilities that must be borne and the expectations that cannot be fulfilled.

As a convinced democrat committed to a form of democracy that far exceeds what is normal today, I offer my book to all those who have neither the time nor the inclination to read a political science treatise many hundreds of pages long. Politicians seldom have the time for this unless they have just lost an election. I have therefore tried to write a book that is short and easy to understand by leaving out footnotes and too much background information.

Another reason for the absence of footnotes is the fact that it would be difficult for me today to retrace the sources from which I obtained the information over the decades. It certainly stems from a great number of books and articles I have read, but also from many conversations I have had with scientists from various fields or with politicians at both national and international level. Thus I have limited myself in Chapter 1 to illustrating for the reader the personal experiences that have shaped my conception of the state. I have been able to look at the state from many different angles: as a head of state; as a politician, who had to win referenda in a direct democracy; as a businessman active not only in his own state but also in different continents; and as an amateur historian fascinated by the evolution of humanity and the influence of military technology, transportation, and the economy on the size of states. In Chapters 2 to 9, I single out those forces that I believe have influenced human history in the past and in all probability will continue to do so in the future. These include, among other things, religions, ideologies, military technology, economics, and systems of transportation. Some readers may find that about seventy pages of human history is too short and others may find it too long.

Readers who are less interested in history can skip Chapters 1 to 9 and concentrate on Chapters 10 to 13. Proposals are explained therein that serve to make the traditional democratic constitutional state more democratic and more efficient. I also discuss possible strategies on how to realize worldwide the modern democratic constitutional state in the third millennium. The objective of the third millennium must be to transform all states into peaceful service companies that are at the service of humanity. Humanity should no longer serve the state and have its existence threatened by wars or other state measures. This is the purpose of the draft constitution for the state of the third millennium that is included as an appendix and is commented on in Chapter 11.

1. The right to self-determination— a personal conviction

When I was a high school student in the 1950s, I became interested in the factors that led to the war in Algeria. I just could not understand why the right to self-determination applied to a mere twenty thousand Liechtensteiners but not to the various ethnic groups in Algeria, some of which numbered in the millions.

I was confronted with the same problem in Spain in 1966 during the time of Franco. I was an economics student doing a bank internship in the Basque region of Spain. Diplomacy was never really a strength of mine, and in discussions I could not resist the temptation to suggest that if the right to self-determination applied to the small number of Liechtensteiners, it should also apply to the Basques. My Basque friends were pleased but my Spanish friends were more diplomatic than I was. They would have been justified in responding that if self-determination did not apply to the Basques, then there was no reason to apply it to the Liechtensteiners either.

If one is born into a family like mine, one is usually interested in history and is internationally minded. History and world politics were discussed and criticized in the family, and from a certain age the children were in a position not simply to follow discussions but also to participate in them. It had been clear to family members for quite some time that the model of a hereditary monarchy whose authority to rule was based on religious legitimation or "the grace of God" had had its day.

The only difference in opinion related to whether this model had ceased to be workable in the 19th century or even earlier. Within the family all were in agreement that ideological forms of legitimation like nationalism or socialism were cul-de-sacs of human development. Despite its fundamental problems, democracy appeared to be the only credible alternative to "the grace of God." However, during my youth there was no complete agreement about which model of democracy was the best.

Witnessing the decades of decolonization was a fascinating experience for me as a young man. Unfortunately, sooner or later, all the models for democracy and economic development in the new nations proved to be political and economic failures, regardless of whether they followed the British, French, or American example. The few successes, such as Singapore or South Korea, were the exceptions that proved the rule. Political analysts and economists had almost unanimously predicted dim prospects for Singapore when it obtained independence. For a long time after the Korean War, South Korea was considered a problem case without a future. At the time, in the 1960s, experts predicted a bright future for the states of Asia, Africa, and Latin America that were rich in raw materials. Unfortunately, nationalism and socialism in those states have destroyed not only every experiment in democracy but also, as a general rule, the economy.

A further problem was that the post-colonial states were almost without exception artificial creations. Colonial powers drew borders without consulting the affected populations. This resulted in states with very heterogeneous populations or so-called multi-ethnic states. The historic Habsburg monarchy is an interesting parallel: a classic example of a multi-ethnic state, it intermingled many languages, races, and religions in very close proximity. Languages were different from one village to the next; one village was Catholic and its neighbor Protestant or Orthodox; and Jewish minorities lived within these communities. Nationalism destroyed the Habsburg Empire and drove Europe into the political catastrophes of the 20th century. Nationalism continues to exert its destructive influence, both inside and outside Europe; minorities are suppressed, expelled, or exterminated.

My family's intense analysis of the problems of the Habsburg Empire, as well as our interest in similar multicultural and multi-religious empires and states throughout history, are understandable in the light of our close and amicable relations with the Habsburg family over the centuries. Already under the Babenberg dukes (predecessors of the Habsburgs), my family had a strong position in what are today eastern Austria and the Moravian region of the Czech Republic. When the Babenberg family died out in the 13th century, we supported the Habsburgs. Only during a brief period in the 15th and 16th centuries did we have religious and political differences with them. In addition to the political connections, the two families were also personally related. My grandmother, for instance, was a younger sister of Franz Ferdinand, who was next in line to the throne when he was assassinated in Sarajevo. We often discussed in my family what political reforms might have saved the Habsburg Empire from its demise. With the example of the Swiss on our doorstep, robust democracy at the local level and political decentralization were the obvious solutions. The political decentralization of the Habsburg Empire was proposed by the young Emperor Charles I after the death of Emperor Franz Joseph I during the First World War, when it was unfortunately already too late.

In the second half of the 20th century even Switzerland, the model democracy, faced a minority problem in the canton of Bern, where the Swiss capital is located. Bern is one of the largest and most important cantons in Switzerland. In the Jura region of the canton, the French-speaking Catholics felt politically and economically disadvantaged compared to the German-speaking Protestant majority of Bern. The French-speaking population aspired to greater autonomy for the Jura region, but they met with resistance from the German-speaking majority. The conflict escalated: there were bomb attacks, and radical elements wanted Jura to become part of France. The Confederal Swiss Government intervened in the internal cantonal problem and mediated a solution in 1974. The French-speaking regions of the canton of Bern voted for Jura to become its own canton. The decision was supported by a clear majority, although some French-speaking communities chose to remain in the canton of Bern. Over the years the political and economic developments in Jura exceeded expectations, and several French-speaking communities that had remained with Bern decided to join the canton of Jura. This peaceful and democratic solution, after such violent conflict, was for me an impressive example of a successful experiment in self-determination at the local level.

In addition to the historical and political interests that I inherited from my family, my studies of economics and law at the University of St. Gallen in Switzerland led me to a rigorous analysis of the planned communist economies in Eastern Europe. In my family we were mainly convinced that the communist systems in Eastern Europe would sooner or later collapse. The only question was when and how it would happen. My father, Prince Franz Josef II, was convinced that the Soviet Empire would fall prior to the turn of the millennium and that it would be a peaceful process. In view of the high oil prices since the beginning of the 1970s, from which the Soviet Union benefited substantially, I personally believed that the economic collapse would probably only take place after the turn of the millennium and possibly after a major nuclear war. My father turned out to be right. The collapse of the Soviet Empire and the Soviet Union started in 1989, and the people of Eastern Europe were able to free themselves from their socialist dictatorships.

Influenced by the collapse of the Habsburg monarchy and its unfortunately negative consequences, I pondered how the Soviet Union could be reformed in order to prevent a collapse. I concluded that only radical reforms can save large multi-ethnic states from disintegration.

In contrast to the Habsburg monarchy, a reform of the Soviet Union required a complete economic reorganization with the introduction of a market economy. Nevertheless, there were parallels between the two empires. Both were multi-ethnic states with significant minority populations. A breakup along the often haphazardly drawn borders of provinces or regional republics would lead inevitably to new minority problems, bringing the potential danger of ethnic cleansing and civil war. However, as long as minorities are not infected by the sickness of nationalism or incited to violence by religious fanatics, they can live together in peace for centuries. Indeed, experience throughout the world shows that a diverse mix of minorities can be a considerable enrichment for culture and trade.

When the crisis of the Soviet Union became unmistakable in the 1980s, it appeared to me that the only possibility of saving it would be the right to self-determination at a local level; a reorientation of the central government solely to matters of foreign affairs, defense policy, internal security, and the law; and a radical program of privatization and rapid integration into the world economy. President Gorbachev never recognized the necessity of such radical reforms. However, even if he had, his chances of success in implementing them would have been minimal. He would first have had to use the military and the KGB (secret police) to oust the Communist Party, and then turn the KGB against the military in order to pursue a radical reduction in armaments expenditure. Finally, the only way he could have built a constitutional state would have been to dissolve the KGB. Nevertheless, President Gorbachev's achievements were truly great and historic. Not only did he dissolve the Soviet Union more or less peacefully, but he also prevented a major civil war that could have escalated into a nuclear conflict. I sincerely hope that historians in the future will honor the major achievements and statesmanship of President Gorbachev and of the other leading Soviet politicians of that time.

During the second half of the 20th century, Canada also had a political problem with the French-speaking minority in Québec. Nearly half of Québec's population wanted independence, but this would have meant problems for the English-speaking and indigenous native American minorities in Québec who wanted to remain within Canada. At that time I had the opportunity of discussing with Canadians a possible solution to the problem based on the right of self-determination at local level. Under this proposal, a relatively narrow strip of land along the St. Lawrence River, where most of the French-speaking population lives, would have become independent. The larger part of Québec, which is richer in natural resources and includes the city of Montréal, would have remained within Canada. Under these conditions, independence would have lost much of its appeal for the French-speaking minority. Since then certain concessions to the French-speaking minority seem to have solved the problem at least to some extent.

At almost the same time, a counter-example could be witnessed in Yugoslavia, where, particularly in Serbia and Croatia, the leadership failed completely. Yugoslavia collapsed into a long, bloody civil war and a period of ethnic cleansing. Even though Yugoslavia was politically and economically closer to the West than to the Soviet Union, this catastrophe still occurred.

From the very beginning, the actions of the international community in Yugoslavia were mostly ill-fated. The highest priorities were non-intervention and the inviolability of all existing borders, with no clear concept of how to prevent the imminent civil war. When the first shots were fired, the international community began to recognize the sovereignty of the individual republics within their existing borders, although they were aware that, with the exception of Slovenia, these borders were artificial and extremely problematic. Yugoslavia might have been saved and civil war averted, had the international community insisted that the sovereignty of Yugoslavia and the inviolability of its borders would only be recognized on the condition that Yugoslavia respect the right of self-determination at the local level. Under pressure from, and with the support of, the international community, the functions of the Yugoslav state could have been reduced to their core competencies, and at the end of the process the European Union (EU) could have offered membership to a fundamentally reformed Yugoslavia as an incentive. The borders of the constituent republics could have been redrawn to correspond more closely with the needs and desires of the local population. These constituent republics could have assumed important functions in social, economic, and specific legal spheres, which had previously been the responsibility of the central government. The international community could still have recognized the sovereignty of these constituent republics, if the Yugoslav central government ignored its recommendation to grant self-determination at the local level. Sadly, ethnic cleansing came once again to European soil, and Europe only looked on, which damaged the credibility of Europe worldwide.

There was one further factor that made me realize early on that states would be much more exposed to centrifugal forces in the next hundred years than in the previous century, and that the danger of their disintegrating either peacefully or through civil war would grow. When I completed my studies at St. Gallen in the 1960s, the predominant view of both private corporations and states was "the bigger the better." A state like Liechtenstein, not only small, but also a monarchy, was seen as a curious relic from a bygone age with no future. Europe, it was argued, could only survive politically and economically through unification. Since I was expected to become the head of state of just such a small country, I had to ask myself whether it was sensible to prepare for a job that had no future. I therefore analyzed intensely the question of the relevance of the small state.

Throughout history there have been periods and regions in which small states have dominated and others in which large states have prevailed. Prior to the Roman Empire, small states like the Greek city-states controlled the political landscape in Europe, and after the fall of the Roman Empire, Europe was characterized primarily by small states until the end of the Middle Ages. Subsequently, the trend moved again towards larger and more centralized states. It was assumed that this trend would reach its peak with the integration of the European states into the EU.

As an economics student, however, it occurred to me that Liechtenstein's economic success after the Second World War directly contradicted the widespread belief in "the bigger the better." When I confronted experts with this contrast between theory and practice, they replied that the finance industry, tourism, and postage stamps were the reasons for Liechtenstein's economic upturn. Yet this was not strictly true. Tourism had some significance for this small country before the Second World War but collapsed during the war and played only a subordinate role thereafter. Postage stamps, compared to larger countries, made a disproportionately large contribution to the national budget and helped to keep taxes low, but that still did not account for the postwar upturn. And although, soon after the First World War, Liechtenstein had tried to support the finance sector with low taxes and favorable legal regulations, success was limited by Europe's restrictive foreign exchange policies between the wars. The annexation of Austria in 1938 by the Third Reich then led to a withdrawal of foreign capital because there was widespread fear of a German military occupation of Liechtenstein.

A closer look at Liechtenstein's statistics in the 1960s clearly reveals that industry was the real motor of the country's economic upturn after the Second World War. Liechtenstein's industry had its roots in the second half of the 19th century, when a customs agreement was reached with the Habsburg monarchy. Low taxes, low wages, and a well-trained labor force made Liechtenstein a relatively attractive location for the neighboring Swiss textile industry, which supplied the large market of the Habsburg Empire. With the First World War and the fall of the Habsburg monarchy, Liechtenstein's small industry lost its market and had to be restructured around the Swiss market because high tariffs and currency restrictions made exports to the rest of Europe difficult. This reorientation towards the Swiss market was only possible because Switzerland was willing to conclude a favorable customs agreement with Liechtenstein, similar to the previous agreement with the Habsburg monarchy.

Following the Second World War, Western Europe did not repeat the error made after the First World War, when individual states had allowed nationalistic impulses to seal off their markets. Last but not least, pressure from the United States liberalized European trade, especially in the industrial sector both within Western Europe and with the United States and Canada.

New markets opening worldwide in the industrial sector offered unexpected opportunities for little Liechtenstein, whose industrial experience, though modest, was nevertheless nearly a century old. Liechtenstein attracted foreign investment and encouraged domestic entrepreneurial talents with its well-trained population, low taxation, legal framework, and hardly any state bureaucracy, which it simply could not afford at that time. Liechtenstein was also attractive to highly skilled personnel from Germany and Austria, who faced an uncertain political and economic future in the wake of the Second World War. Guest workers from Liechtenstein had gone to work in Switzerland until 1945, but soon the Swiss were coming to work in Liechtenstein instead.

The more closely I studied Liechtenstein's economic development and the many small successful companies that had sprung up after the Second World War both in Liechtenstein and elsewhere, the more firmly I was convinced that the prevailing belief in "the bigger, the better" was fundamentally false.

For hundreds of years before the Second World War, trade over long distances was expensive and difficult, due to the high cost of transportation, unsafe trade routes, poor communication, high customs duties, technical regulations, and other obstacles. Consequently, larger states had a decisive competitive advantage over smaller states because, unlike the latter, they could produce virtually everything within their own borders. Internal trade barriers could be abolished, and monopoly profits could be earned from sought-after raw materials or other products for which production was regionally limited. As transportation over water was much cheaper than by land, states like France built expensive waterways and covered part of their country with an intricately constructed canal system, so reducing transportation costs further. Other states like Great Britain had a natural advantage because, like ancient Greece, every economically important region was easily accessible by sea. The seafaring states were the most successful builders of colonial empires. Colonial empires made industrialization easier by offering large markets and nearly every raw material within their borders.

At the beginning of the Industrial Revolution, smaller countries, and especially land-locked ones, were doubly disadvantaged. On the one hand, they had to import raw materials at high cost, and on the other, industrial mass production demanded a large volume of potential sales that domestic markets could not generally provide. Exports, which could have financed imports, were hardly competitive because of trade barriers and high transport costs to the markets of the large states. Whenever cheaper, and often better, industrial goods produced in large quantities replaced old handicrafts, small states found themselves in an increasingly critical economic, political, social, and military situation. From the end of the Middle Ages until the end of the Second World War, the trend toward larger states appeared to be inevitable for economic and military reasons.

As far as I can judge, this trend toward larger states was not only interrupted following the Second World War, but had turned again toward small states, not only for economic but also for military reasons, as I shall try to explain later. The Austrian professor Leopold Kohr (1909–94) and some of his friends recognized this early on and coined the phrase "small is beautiful." Nevertheless, for Kohr's group it was not economic or political considerations that inspired this conviction, but rather the human dimension, which in their opinion had been lost in the growth of large states and corporations. Professor Kohr was a fan of Liechtenstein, and after the Second World War he often visited the country. I had the honor and the pleasure of making his acquaintance and of having the opportunity to discuss these questions with him.

With the extensive reduction of trade barriers in the so-called western world and the drastic reduction of transportation costs by land through the expansion of road and railroad networks, it became possible even for a small country such as Liechtenstein to import cheaply for the benefit of consumers, as well as to develop a competitive export industry for the benefit of workers. One further factor was also in our favor. Industrial development moved away from cheap mass production towards smaller, more flexible, and innovative industrial units in which products could be manufactured at higher profit margins. After the Second World War, Liechtenstein was ideally placed to exploit these opportunities and to industrialize rapidly.

Large states had not only lost their economic advantage over small states like Liechtenstein, but were even at a disadvantage. Their industries relied mainly on domestic or colonial markets for purchases and sales. This usually meant, first, that their purchase prices were too high; second, that they missed the newest innovations on the procurement market; third, that they were dependent for their sales on a protected market; and fourth, that they paid little attention to the worldwide development of competition.

Any leader today who still believes that he or she can protect domestic markets with tariffs and trade barriers inflicts dual damage on the economy, first because consumers have to pay higher prices for inferior quality, and second because the workplace is endangered, since both the consumer and the producer must pay higher prices and are at a disadvantage in relation to foreign competition.

Since Liechtenstein could not offer its companies any significant domestic market in the industrial sector, they had to concentrate from the very beginning on European or even world markets. Averaged over recent years, over 40 percent of Liechtenstein's industrial exports go outside Europe, over 10 percent go to Switzerland, which can almost be considered a domestic market, and the rest of Europe accounts for 40 percent.

A further factor, namely the lack of labor in Liechtenstein, forced successful Liechtenstein entrepreneurs to develop their own subsidiaries abroad. The reservoir of labor in Liechtenstein and in the neighboring regions of Switzerland and Austria was rapidly exhausted, and companies began recruiting guest workers. By the 1960s the number of foreigners had risen to over 30 percent of the population; it became a political problem and led to regulations restricting the hiring of foreign labor. Labor costs and salaries rose swiftly. Automation and streamlining offset some of these costs, but companies planning to grow had to relocate part of their production, sales, research, and administration abroad. Liechtenstein companies soon employed more workers abroad than domestically.

I was able to follow this development very closely and compare it with what was happening in larger states, both within and outside Europe, which I knew as a result of my own entrepreneurial activity. By the late 1970s I was convinced of the overall shift in favor of small states, at least in economic terms. The collapse of colonial empires was not just due to politics. It was above all the liberalization of world trade that reduced significantly the economic competitiveness of colonial empires. States that could not integrate with the global economy had no future, no matter how large they were. As time progressed, colonies increasingly became an economic and political burden. With the globalization of the world economy, forces were released that could put the existence of many states in doubt.

However positive this development was for a small state like Liechtenstein, provided it maintained its successful policies, I recognized that these trends posed dangers to world peace. As I have already mentioned, I considered the Soviet Union to be in particular danger. By 1990, when Liechtenstein obtained membership of the United Nations (UN), the disintegration of the Soviet Union appeared as imminent as that of Yugoslavia. The time seemed right to combine my first speech to the UN General Assembly with an initiative for the right to self-determination. In 1992, in an address at the Woodrow Wilson School of Public and International Affairs at Princeton University, Princeton, New Jersey, I outlined the possibility of a new interpretation of self-determination as a means to avoid bloodshed and conflict. Shortly thereafter I established a research program there, which in 2000 became the Liechtenstein Institute on Self-Determination. Princeton University was in my opinion the ideal location for such an institute because of its proximity to the UN headquarters in New York. Professor Woodrow Wilson, before becoming president of the United States, was president of Princeton University and was an important supporter of the right to self-determination after the First World War. Professor Wolfgang Danspeckgruber, with whom I had discussed these issues since the early 1980s, became director of the institute. A series of conferences was organized in Princeton and Liechtenstein, to which international experts and representatives from UN member states were invited, and a UN draft convention on the right of self-determination through self-administration was formulated and published.

The topic and the draft proposal met with strong interest but, as might be expected, also considerable opposition. Some states saw in such a convention the opportunity to decentralize and thereby save states that were in danger of collapse. Others feared that such a clear definition of the right to self-determination, a right already established as part of the UN Charter but never precisely defined, would in fact hasten the disintegration of many states. Today, the right to self-determination remains a central but still unfulfilled principle of the UN.

In light of the difficulties in reaching a consensus on this problem at the UN, I decided not to pursue the matter any further there for the time being. Another reason for my decision was the growing discussion about the constitution in Liechtenstein regarding the position of the monarchy. On the one hand, I feared that the criticism leveled by my political opponents, namely, that the monarchy failed the test of democratic legitimation, would sooner or later be used against the Liechtenstein initiative for the right to self-determination in the UN. On the other hand, I saw the opportunity not only of legitimizing the monarchy democratically, but also of making the right to self-determination at the local level explicitly part of Liechtenstein's constitution, and in a form that went even further than what was proposed in the UN draft convention. Following the reform of the constitution, Liechtenstein could again present the initiative for the right to self-determination from a much more credible position, should a more favorable opportunity arise at the UN.

In the meantime, the Liechtenstein Institute at Princeton University could focus on educating students, conducting research, holding conferences, and issuing publications that address this question.

As I have already mentioned, the right to self-determination is firmly established in the UN Charter and should be discussed not just in a narrow circle of political experts, diplomats, and politicians, but also among the general public. I find it problematic that world leaders try continually to treat the right to self-determination as an impractical theory that can never be applied in practice. Even for the most powerful world leaders, this will cause many more problems in the long run than if the international community agrees on a well-defined right to self-determination.

I hope that my remarks have succeeded in helping the reader understand why my family and I are supporters of democracy and the right to self-determination. We in the Princely House wish to provide the head of state in Liechtenstein only for as long as it is the wish of the majority of the population and provided that we have democratic legitimation. It is not the size of the state that matters, or whether the state is a monarchy, oligarchy or democracy, but rather whether the state serves the people or not. In principle it is all the same to us in the Princely House whether the Principality of Liechtenstein is one hundred and sixty square kilometers, or just sixteen. Far more important for us is the question of whether the people of Liechtenstein can live in happiness and freedom.

Even if it were only sixteen square kilometers (about six square miles), the Principality of Liechtenstein would still be almost ten times the size of the Principality of Monaco, where some 30,000 people live in freedom and happiness. The Principality of Monaco could probably only expand its population by expanding its territory proportionally; the Principality of Liechtenstein, on the other hand, could greatly multiply its population within its existing boundaries, with unlimited immigration. Unfortunately, neither one of these scenarios is possible. We should therefore devote our efforts to the creation of numerous small principalities throughout the world, where people can live in happiness and freedom. The large states need not be destroyed in order to achieve this goal. Rather, they must be convinced of the need to decentralize politically in order to bring democracy and self-determination into their smallest political units, namely local communities, be they villages or cities.

2. The origins of the state

When, where, and how the first state was born is unknown. Moreover, political experts and historians are not in total agreement about what should be called a state and what should not. For the purpose of this book, I have used a very simple definition of the state as a geographical area that is more or less defined, with a population that in the majority has accepted a central authority or has been forced to accept such an authority over a long period of time. This central authority has to be in a position to defend its territory and its population against external aggression, either with diplomacy or with weapons.

Defined thus simply, the state has its origin in a time period when humanity consisted of hunters and gatherers. There are no written documents from this time, but we can study the hunter-gatherer societies that have survived into our time. Some historians might argue that the first state was born much later, in the agrarian period—perhaps with the Sumerians or the Egyptians—but certainly not with rather primitive nomads.

On the basis of my chosen definition of the state, however, hunter-gatherers without permanent residence are nevertheless able to create states. Nomadic tribes usually control a particular territory. The borders of the territories of hunter-gatherer societies were perhaps not as well defined as in the later agrarian period, but border disputes have existed throughout human history up to the present time.

This glance far back into history makes it easier to understand the origins and varieties of states. If states or state-like organizations have shaped human history not only over the last few thousand years but over hundreds of thousands of years, humanity should be much more receptive to the order of a state than if the state were a more recent phenomenon.

Those hunter-gatherer tribes that have survived until today usually have a chief in their village or tribal community. The office of chief is either hereditary or elective. One can assume that as early as the Stone Age there were hereditary and elected chiefs or monarchs. In larger communities today, the monarch is supported by a council, the membership of which is decided by age, through election, or on the basis of some other criteria. Monarchic, oligarchic, and democratic elements have probably existed in human society for much longer than the last few thousand years.

The ancient Greeks classified the different types of states and gave them the names of monarchy, oligarchy, and democracy. In ancient Greece, monarchy meant the rule of a single person, the monarch, and the expression was not restricted to hereditary monarchy. Some monarchs have always been elected: the Holy Roman Emperor, for instance, was a monarch elected for life. A president might be considered a monarch elected for a limited period of time.

The rule of the few was known as oligarchy. Most people are not as familiar with this term as they are with monarchy and democracy, which are often and wrongly seen as being opposites. Quite early on the term oligarchy obtained a somewhat negative connotation, and oligarchs preferred to be called aristocrats, which means in Greek "the rule of the best." As a member of an old aristocratic family, I have nothing against such a term, but it would be historically unjust to favor oligarchy over monarchy and democracy. Nevertheless, one cannot stress enough that in each state the monarch, elected or hereditary, and the people, have to delegate a number of important tasks to the oligarchy, in order to ensure that the state can function. These tasks can be in government, administration, defense, economy, the legal system, or the formulation and resolution of laws, for example by a parliament. The oligarchs, be they members of government, parliament, the courts, the administration, or political parties, could be described as the technocrats of state power. Without an oligarchy the duties of the state towards its population cannot be fulfilled over a long period of time. The oligarchy is therefore the strongest element in the state, but if it does not fulfill the interests of the state, it loses the trust of the people or of the monarch and the existence of the state is jeopardized.

Democracy means the rule of the people (*demos*). However, from antiquity until the American Revolution in the 18th century, the prevalent wisdom was that democracy is only possible in political units which are sufficiently small for the people to be able to gather to discuss and resolve together important questions of common interest. It was also generally believed that democracy leads to arbitrary rule, because people change their opinion too often, and that the rule of law is therefore not possible in a democracy over a long period of time. The fear was that democracy would be the first step towards anarchy and dissolution of the state order.

Anarchy was seen as an unstable and dangerous condition that might threaten the very existence of the people. In antiquity, it was thought that no type of state could remain stable over long periods of time: sooner or later monarchy would be followed by oligarchy, oligarchy by democracy, and democracy by anarchy; if the state wanted to survive, it had to be saved by a monarch, and the whole cycle started once again. Only mixed constitutions that combined monarchic, oligarchic, and democratic elements into a harmonic symbiosis were thus considered to be relatively stable. On this basis Cicero praised the Roman Republic and Montesquieu the English type of state.

For thousands of years, religion was an important element in the creation and preservation of the state. It has had a dominant role in human history because a certain religiousness is probably part of our genetic background. Illiterate tribes had and still have laws that are passed on orally from generation to generation. There is a need for legitimation of these laws and for the authority that has to execute them, so that they are accepted by the people over a long period of time. This legitimation in the eyes of the people can be achieved essentially in two ways: religious legitimation, where law and authority are basically given by God or the gods; or democratic legitimation, where the majority of the people entitled to vote makes decisions either directly or indirectly.

3. The role of religion in the formation of the state

Throughout human history religion has been the usual means of legitimating the law and state authority. Even in the old democracies, religious beliefs were the foundation for the law and state authority. In the various republics in Greece and in the Roman Republic, religious ceremonies had a central role to play in the state. The state treasury was kept in a temple and each state occasion was accompanied by religious ceremonies. For the Greeks in antiquity and the Europeans of the Middle Ages, religion was an important link that connected people despite all the wars they were waging against each other.

Why has religion played and does it still play such a central role in human history? Apart from other explanations, human evolution might help explain why humans seem to have an inborn religious sense.

In animals social behavior is guided to a large extent by innate instincts. Social behavior—from the breeding and raising of the next generation, through group behavior, to the defending of territory—is crucial to the survival of a species. It is not so much the interests and survival of the individual that really matter as the genes and social behavior that promote the survival of the group or species in a particular environment. One speaks about the egoism of the genes, which can to some extent conflict with the egoism of the individual. In the animal kingdom this conflict is decided in favor of the group and the species by behavior that is guided by instincts. The higher the intelligence, the more the individual can realize that his instinctive behavior might be good for the survival of the species, but a disadvantage for him personally. Everybody will agree that the social behavior of humans is guided to a much greater extent by intelligence than is the case with apes, despite our genetic proximity to them.

It seems that evolution, nature, or God has—through the inborn religiousness of humanity—tipped this balance between instinctive social behavior and intelligence back in the direction of the preservation of the species, to the disadvantage of the egoism of the individual. If we take evolution as an explanation, inborn religiousness has partly overtaken the role of instinct through the increasing intelligence of mankind. Humans with a high intelligence and a lower degree of religiousness have apparently had fewer descendants than others throughout the course of history. It is assumed that in the Roman Empire, Christianity spread through a higher birthrate rather than through conversions. States with the relevant statistics usually show higher birthrates for religious families.

The question of whether evolution has indeed caused a genetic embedding of religiosity in the brain will perhaps be answered one day by neuroscience or biogenetic research. Such research has already produced surprising results. Today, it is possible to measure and localize brain activity, which develops due to emotions or the cognitive process, by exposing the brain to magnetic fields. Perhaps one day, we may even discover that emotions caused by religion and ideology take place in similar areas of the brain. That would indeed mean that ideology represents an "ersatzreligion."

Besides having fewer surviving descendants, those tribes ruled by non-religious groups might have been less competitive because religions convey a belief in life after death as well as in a compensating justice. This compensating justice after death can be of divine nature or a law of nature, for instance, in Buddhism, where reincarnation plays a central role.

There will always be intelligent individuals whose innate religiousness is very weak. Some of them will try to take advantage of those people whose behavior continues to be guided either by instincts or religiousness. As long as these people remain in a minority and do not dominate a society or a state through their egoistic, non-religious behavior, society and the state will survive. It becomes problematic when those people rule the state or shape society and persecute or suppress religions. It normally does not take long for such a state to collapse and be replaced by another one. The Soviet Union is a good example, even if this was not the only reason for its collapse.

For an intelligent person who is convinced that there is no life after death and no compensating justice after death, the best strategy might be to achieve the maximum gain in his short life here on earth. The barriers of religion and morality disappear. The law is only a deterrent as long as there is a danger that transgressing it will be noticed and that the consequent punishment could outweigh the potential advantages. Communism, which tried actively to suppress religion, was a failure. However, a materialistic ideology which values self-realization and the amusement of the individual is also problematic. The materialistic, fun society of Western Europe, which sees religion as a relic of the past without meaning for the future, might also turn out to be a failure. Communism and the materialistic society share a low birth rate. Before communism died out, it collapsed economically. In the welfare state, the state bears the cost for sickness and old age. The family and raising children are often seen as an unnecessary burden. The materialistic society is an economic success, but produces few heirs to inherit the wealth it creates.

A society without religion not only produces fewer or no heirs but may lay the foundation for a state that is dominated by religion. History provides a number of examples of a new religion or religious movement taking over a state in which the old religion had lost its strength. In many of these cases, tolerance for other religions or non-religious groups was the first victim. Those of the intelligentsia who do not believe in life after death and compensating justice should commit themselves—in their own interest—to ensuring that religions still play an important role in the state of the future. On the other hand, the state has to require respect for the freedom of conscience of each person, whether he believes in religion or not. The problem of the fun society can only be solved if one succeeds in connecting the market economy focused on consumption by the individual with the inherited religiousness of humanity and turns it into a fortunate symbiosis for the welfare of humanity.

Apart from intelligence, a fortunate mixture of individuality and social behavior distinguishes humanity from most animal species. An animal species of highly intelligent individuals, whose parents do not invest any time in raising their descendants and who only occasionally meet for breeding, is not able to build a modern civilization, which demands complex cooperation among many individuals. If a typical loner in the animal kingdom, such as the bear, were much more intelligent than humans, humans would still be far superior to the bear because of their social behavior. On the other hand, a highly intelligent animal species with a strong herd instinct that fully dominates the behavior of the individual would be just as unable to build a modern civilization. It would be a very conservative society with hardly any freedom and progress. Humanity is characterized by the fact that people have a high degree of individuality and intelligence, which gives them the freedom to experiment and research, but also the ability to pass on the knowledge gained to the group and their descendants. The development of language and later on of writing accelerated this process in a decisive way.

It was certainly one of the major challenges of human evolution to find the right balance between egoistic individuality and social behavior. The herd instinct and the egoistic anti-social behavior of many people are the result of this evolution. Obviously, we need both of them, otherwise human society either falls apart or stagnates. Neither the herd instinct nor the egoistic behavior of the individual should dominate the state and society; rather, a very fine balance has to be found between the two.

This unique combination of intelligence and social behavior made it possible for people to settle in all climatic zones, from the tropical rainforest to the frozen deserts of the Arctic region. On top of that, humans can organize themselves according to their needs, from a small tribe with a few dozen individuals to large states with millions of inhabitants. States with several hundred thousands or even millions of inhabitants are, as far as we know, a rather recent phenomenon in human history. They have their origins in the agrarian era, because agriculture and cattle breeding allowed a much higher density of population in a given area than the hunter-gatherer societies of the Stone Age.

During the transition from the hunter-gatherer society to the agrarian age, state structures did not change much initially, despite the fact that some states had much larger populations. In the larger states, the monarchic and oligarchic elements were strengthened to the detriment of the democratic element. In states with several hundred thousand people, it was simply not possible to gather the whole population and to vote on issues. Since at best only a small part of the population could read and write, written ballots were not possible. Religious legitimation for the law, and for the state authority which had to execute the law, became more and more important. Most readers will know from the Old Testament about the tablets with the Ten Commandments given to Moses by God. However, the religious legitimation of law and state authority is not confined to the Jewish and Christian cultures, but was also the rule in the ancient world. Monarchs tried to trace their ancestors back to the gods. Well into the 20th century, for example, many Japanese believed the Imperial House of Japan to be of divine origin.

Religious minorities became a problem for states that sought their legitimation in religion. In the ancient world this problem was often solved by integrating the religion of the minorities into the religion of the dominant population. Before a war, the people asked their own gods for help and prayed and offered sacrifices to them. Defeat and subjugation were a sign that the gods of the enemy were stronger, and, as a result, the subjugation of their own gods to the foreign god and integration of their religion into a foreign religion was usually possible without too much difficulty. The Roman Empire is a good example of such a religious policy, which was successful for centuries. In ancient Rome there were temples dedicated to a large number of foreign religions and foreign gods. To strengthen the authority of imperial rule in the Roman Empire, the emperor was elevated to a divine position. This was no problem as long as the foreign religions accepted the predominance of the Roman gods in the hierarchy of the gods.

Difficulties started with the Jews and the Christians, who believed in one god and did not accept any other gods. The idea of a divine emperor was totally unacceptable to them. That brought into question the religious legitimation of the emperor, the state authority, and state laws. This explains, to a large extent, the difficult relationship between the Roman Empire and the Jews, as well as the repeated persecution of the Christians. The Roman Empire viewed the Jewish religion as the smaller danger because the Jewish religion did not seek to make converts, unlike Christianity. Furthermore, the Jews lived in an area on the periphery of the Roman Empire, whereas Christianity spread rapidly into the center of the empire in Rome. There were conversions not only among the lower classes but also among the upper classes, which made Christianity even more threatening in the minds of the imperial authorities.

Besides the higher birthrate noted earlier, the rapid spread of Christianity in the Roman Empire can probably be attributed to two other factors. First, as already mentioned, the pantheon of gods in the old Roman religion increased continuously for political reasons, which led to a loss of credibility of the old religion in the eyes of a large part of the population. The behavior of some of the Roman emperors did not exactly support belief in a system that turned the emperor into a divine being. Second, the close connection between state and religion invariably led to a situation where politics misused religion. Mistakes by state leaders and bad laws then weakened both state and religion, a problem that can hardly be avoided when law and state authority are based on religious legitimation.

In the year 313 the Edict of Milan, issued by Emperor Constantine I, gave the Christians freedom of religion. The old Roman religion lost its position as a state religion and became just one religion among others within the context of the new religious freedom. It was probably little noticed at the beginning that the state authority thus lost its religious legitimation, because the power of habit gives legitimation for a limited period of time after the original legitimation has been lost.

Emperor Constantine and his immediate successors probably did not realize the loss of legitimation for law and state authority; otherwise they might have replaced the old religion immediately with Christianity. However, Christian teachings are not necessarily compatible with making Christianity into a state religion. Christ mentioned several times that His empire is not of this world and that one should give the emperor what is due to him and God what is due to God. A democratic legitimation of law and state authority was never taken into consideration, for reasons mentioned above.

Signs of decay in the Roman Empire convinced Emperor Theodosius approximately sixty-five years later finally to declare Christianity the state religion. The old temples were destroyed or turned into Christian churches and other religions were suppressed. Not much later the old Roman Empire broke apart. Christianity survived, but split. The model of a state religion with close connection between church and state survived in the Byzantine Empire. This concept survived in the Orthodox Church even after the downfall of the Byzantine Empire.

The popes in Rome developed another model. With the creation of the papal state, the popes were able to maintain considerable independence from emperors, kings, and other secular rulers. In the Middle Ages the popes even extended their influence over the secular powers. There was a latent conflict between church and state, and between the pope and the emperor or king. The open question was whether the secular power would rule primarily over the spiritual power, as was the case with few exceptions in all those states that based their legitimation on religion, or whether the Catholic Church would succeed in ruling over the secular power. The difference between the Byzantine Empire and Western Europe was that Western Europe was politically divided, and individual rulers were not interested in strengthening the emperor or the different kings; it was therefore possible for the pope to find allies to defend his political independence. At a time when democratic legitimation was restricted to very small political entities, the ruling houses and their laws were dependent on religious legitimation by the pope. In the so-called Holy

Roman Empire, the emperor was elected, but those who elected him were either hereditary monarchs without democratic legitimation or bishops who were usually nominated by the pope.

The contrast between religious power, with a Catholic Church and the pope, on the one hand, and secular power, with the emperor, kings, and dukes etc. on the other, gave medieval Europe political diversity within a common religious and cultural framework. Parallels can be seen in ancient Greece, with the difference that political, economic, and military competition was not restricted to Greece itself but was extended to a whole continent. The exchange of people, new ideas, and products took place not only within Catholic Europe but also with Byzantium, the Islamic world, and the Asian world as far as China.

Europe absorbed many ideas from outside and through intensive competition inside Europe was able rapidly to adapt such ideas, concepts, and products to European needs and to develop them further. Already in the Middle Ages Catholic Europe was militarily superior to the Byzantine and Islamic empires provided that it was more or less united, as it was during the crusades. Looking back, the worldwide European predominance during the second half of the past millennium is not surprising: it had emerged already in the first half of the second millennium.

During the Middle Ages, the Catholic Church played an important role in the economic growth of Europe. Monasteries were the centers of knowledge, medical care, and education. Rulers attracted and settled monasteries through large land grants and other privileges in order to develop backward regions. In addition, the Catholic Church received donations from all sections of the population so that at the end of the Middle Ages the Church was the largest landowner and the largest economic enterprise in Europe.

The influence of the Catholic Church on economic development was, however, not only positive. A skeptical or even negative attitude towards earthly wealth can already be found in the origins of Christianity, as expressed in an often cited sentence of the Bible: "It is easier for a camel to go through the eye of a needle than for a rich man to enter into the kingdom of God" (Matthew 19:24). This had negative influences on the financial and loan business, trade, and other business areas. In addition, a large part of the huge income from church assets and donations from the population was invested in building, decorating, and maintaining churches and monasteries. The purpose of many of these buildings was mainly to pray. This was a very understandable policy for a church that sees its main task as bringing the glory of God nearer to the people here on earth and preparing people for life after death. For the economic development of a state, however, it was not helpful.

The delicate balance between ecclesiastical and secular power led to an extensive separation between church and state, and thus for many parts of the population to freedoms that did not exist in other regions of the world. When this balance was disrupted at the end of the Middle Ages, the areas of freedom survived despite some setbacks, and expanded step by step.

In the 16th century the structure of power in Europe changed substantially. Through clear rules of succession, the ruling families established something like dynastic legitimation. Dynastic legitimation was basically legitimation through the power of habit. The people became used to a certain ruling family, and as long as the ruling family did not weaken itself through incompetence or internal quarrels, it had the support of a large part of the population. This applied not only to the ruling family and the type of state but also to the laws. They had become customary rights, and even for a powerful ruler it became dangerous to break or to change them.

During the same period, the Catholic Church was weakened spiritually and morally by a stronger earthly orientation and some abuses. The call for profound reforms became stronger, leading to the Protestant Reformation. In addition, new discoveries in science slowly changed the concept of the world from that of the Middle Ages. The ruling families of Britain, Northern Europe, and parts of Germany, as well as the Netherlands and Switzerland, used the opportunity to escape from the influence of the Catholic Church, to expropriate and divide the often large properties of the church, and to eliminate the separation of church and state. The king or the queen of England even became the head of the new Anglican Church. These were not always peaceful changes, and they led to the Thirty Years' War, which destroyed large parts of Europe, especially Germany.

The Thirty Years' War ended without a winner and with the exhaustion of the two opponents, the Catholics and the Protestants. The opponents agreed that the ruling families, or in the republics the political leaders, would decide the religious belief of the population: *Cuius regio eius religio* or "whose rule, whose religion." There were some areas where religious tolerance prevailed, but overall Europe split along religious borders. Those who were not willing to accept the religion of the political leadership were suppressed, persecuted, or expelled. In remote areas there was more religious tolerance because the political leadership wanted to keep those areas settled in order to receive at least some limited taxation. This was especially true for the colonies of North America. One hundred years later these colonies would have special relevance for the further development of the concept of a state and the relation between state and religion.

The expropriation of the Catholic Church and the elimination of its political influence led in the Anglican, Protestant and, especially, Calvinist states of Europe to a liberalization of the economy and to increased investments in the productive part of the economy. The result was stronger economic growth in those areas. This also weakened the influence of the Catholic Church on the economy in the Catholic areas of Europe. The Enlightenment, the French Revolution, and the political developments of the 19th century such as liberalism, nationalism, and socialism further weakened the political influence of the Catholic Church.

The religious wars and persecutions in Europe during the 16th and 17th centuries had weakened the influence of religion not only in Catholic but also in Protestant areas—a development that later extended to the Orthodox areas of Europe in the south and east, and still continues today. The more religion and God were put aside, the more the individual came to the center: man, the discoverer of the world and the laws of nature in a huge universe, which had always existed and was not created by God. The religious legitimation of law and state authority became ever weaker over time. As already mentioned, monarchies tried to replace religious legitimation with dynastic legitimation. This development reached its peak in the French monarchy, when King Louis XIV declared "l'état c'est moi," or "I am the state." This attempt to replace religious by dynastic legitimation failed in France with the French Revolution at the end of the 18th century and in the other European states in the 19th and 20th centuries.

In a world where religion has lost its influence and in states with religious freedom, one can understand why religious legitimation cannot remain the intellectual foundation for a state. The question is, however, why dynastic legitimation failed after such a short period of time. The reason is certainly that dynastic legitimation is not an independent but a deductive legitimation that is based either on religious or on democratic legitimation. If one or the other legitimation disappears, sooner or later the dynastic legitimation collapses. The transition from religious to democratic legitimation was a difficult process worldwide that is still not completed and has led humanity into a number of cul-de-sacs.

Most French people will not like to hear it, but the French Revolution of 1789 produced mainly chaos and a bloodbath, as did the Russian Revolution 130 years later. Since the revolution, France has had four monarchies, and has now reached republic number five. The Russian Revolution was the beginning of one of the cruelest dictatorships of human history, which lasted for approximately seventy years. Neither the French nor the Russian Revolution was willing to fulfill its promises of democratically legitimized rule. The French Revolution, the First World War and its consequences, and the Russian Revolution led both in Europe and outside Europe to a situation in which religious legitimation was mostly replaced by the ideological legitimation of nationalism and socialism and not by democratic legitimation. The intellectual contribution of Europe to the beginning of the democratic age should not be underestimated, but without the American Revolution this contribution would probably have remained of theoretical and historical interest. To the detriment of humanity, religious legitimation would have been replaced to an even greater degree by the ideological legitimation of nationalism and socialism.

The transition from the age of the hunter-gatherer to the agrarian age produced very similar state models not only in Europe but also worldwide, nearly all of them based on religious legitimation. Even the American civilizations of the agrarian age, such as the Aztecs, Incas, or Mayas, who were isolated from Europe, Asia, and Africa, developed very similar state models based on religious legitimation, with a divine monarch at the top and an oligarchy that had its legitimation from the monarch and religion. The vast majority of the population had hardly any rights and no influence on state policy. This state model of the agrarian age gradually collapsed in Europe during the second half of the last millennium. This development has now reached all other continents.

The first attempt to replace the religious legitimation of the state with dynastic legitimation failed. The second attempt to replace religious legitimation with the ideologies of nationalism and socialism ended in the greatest bloodbaths of human history. The third attempt to replace religious legitimation with democracy has somehow become stuck halfway. I very much hope humanity will have the courage to go the rest of the way.

4. The size of states and the influence of military technology

The varying size of states has been discussed above. One might imagine that, in principle, states should have an optimal size based on factors such as population and geography. However, this is clearly not the case, as the size of states varies over time and space. There have been times when large, centralized states have dominated, and other times when small or strongly decentralized states were predominant. There are continents where large and small states have coexisted for long periods and others where that has not been the case. At first glance, it would seem that such differences are just quirks of history.

A closer analysis over long periods, however, reveals that a number of factors influence the size of states. Geographic conditions have a role to play. Flat, easily traversable terrain is difficult to defend and simplifies the development of larger states. Mountainous and inaccessible terrain, as well as islands, are easily defended and improve the chances for the survival of small states.

Military technology and transportation systems also play a decisive role. In the Middle Ages, for instance, military technology favored defense, when high city walls provided ample protection and the transportation infrastructure was very poor. Both these factors were optimal for either small states or decentralized ones like the Holy Roman Empire. On the other hand, highly developed siege technologies and efficient transportation systems permitted the development of large, centralized states like the Roman or Chinese empires.

To study how states originated in the Stone Age, in the absence of written records, we must rely on archeology. As far as we can tell, pre-agrarian Stone Age cultures developed only small states with regard to area and population. Nevertheless, there is evidence that extensive trade relations appeared very early. Shells, stone tools, and similar items were traded over great distances.

The emergence of agriculture some ten thousand years ago marks the establishment of small, as yet unfortified cities as trade centers. Shortly thereafter, fortified cities were built in the region stretching from modern Turkey to Egypt in the so-called fertile crescent. These city-states appear to have been frequently at war with one another. The first large empires appeared along great rivers such as the Nile, the Euphrates, and the Tigris. Large rivers permitted shipping routes and thereby trade, irrigation of fields, and a thriving agrarian economy. Transportation by water extended beyond rivers to seas and oceans; naval warfare was another byproduct of these developments. Homer describes the siege of Troy as having lasted for years. Troops had to be transported, relieved, and otherwise supported. The transport of personnel and materials over water was already much cheaper and safer than over land. The first empires in China also arose on the banks of great rivers, although a little later than in the Near East.

The use of horses and the invention of the wheel facilitated land transportation considerably. Nevertheless, road networks existed even before these developments. Native American cultures, which knew neither horses nor wheels, had a well-developed system of roads for trade and military use. The Inca Empire had an extensive network of roads over high mountains and through thick jungle areas.

With favorable geographic conditions, small city-states could survive behind high fortified walls for centuries. The fragmented political landscape of ancient Greece is a good example. However, if one of these small city-states succeeded militarily against any of its neighbors and brought a land or naval transportation system under its control, or created one, it could establish a large empire quite rapidly.

A good example from ancient times is how the Roman Empire came to power. A small city in the middle of a politically fragmented Italy gradually united its neighboring city-states with a combination of diplomatic and military skill, as well as considerable endurance. The Romans recognized early the importance of roads for military expansion and built the most efficient infrastructure the world had ever seen. Once they had conquered Italy and built a dense network of roads, they assembled a huge fleet to conquer the Mediterranean. They constructed still more roads and harbors along the coasts and rivers from

North Africa to England and from Spain to Romania. The Romans controlled this enormous empire with relatively few troops because they could quickly move them from one trouble spot to another. Geographic barriers like the Alps or the Pyrenees, which were difficult obstacles for armies before and after, were quickly overcome and integrated into the empire. A visit to the almost impregnable Jewish fortress, Masada in eastern Israel, gives some insight into the effectiveness of the Roman Empire even on the periphery of the empire. In a region of little economic, political, or strategic importance, the Romans did not hesitate to build an enormous ramp on the mountain leading up to Masada, which finally enabled them to conquer it after a long siege.

After the fall of the Roman Empire other, still larger empires arose, rapidly established by the equestrian armies of Central Asia. Nevertheless, as rapidly as these empires arose, they disappeared again. The horse was ideal for work and transportation across the Asian steppe with its large grazing plains. Equestrian peoples such as the Huns, the Magyars, and the Mongols were optimally situated to perfect cavalry as an instrument of war. In densely populated, agricultural regions like Europe, the Mediterranean, and South Asia, however, horses were a luxury, affordable only by a privileged few. The vast majority of soldiers in these regions were infantry and, compared to the equestrian armies of Central Asia, the cavalries of the Middle Ages were small and far more expensive. The narrow confines of Western Europe were also not ideal for a purely cavalry-based military. For example, many strategically important regions, such as the Alps and the Pyrenees, were mountainous, so a cheap infantry had a military advantage over cavalry. The Habsburg cavalry faced this very problem in Switzerland during the 14th and 15th centuries.

It is interesting to ask why the militarily superior equestrian armies of Asia and their leaders were unable to establish stable empires like Rome's. These empires were often hereditary monarchies in which the line of succession was unclear. This could lead to the division of the empire by the founder's successors, with conflicts tantamount to civil wars, as was the fate suffered by Alexander the Great's empire after his death. The Roman Empire later became a hereditary monarchy, in which the rule of succession was often unclear. Rome, however, had the advantage of a justice system and an oligarchy that could at least govern, and these factors sustained the empire through many crises. Rome's judicial and legislative systems were developed at the time of the republic and gave the empire a political stability even at times when the monarch was incompetent. Rome had another advantage over the empires of central Asia—for long periods its government was legitimized by its religion.

This is perhaps the decisive reason why the equestrian armies of the Arab world succeeded where the Asian armies had failed, namely in establishing an empire that was stable for a long period of time. Islam gave legitimacy to rulers and their governments and also motivated their armies: whoever fell in the righteous war was sure of a place in heaven. Islam was also more tolerant than other religions and this helped their leaders to find allies among groups oppressed by intolerant rulers. Some Christian rulers persecuted not just other religions but even those Christians whom they considered to have strayed from the true beliefs of Christianity. Consequently, there were Christian ethnic groups in the Arabian peninsula and the Near East who supported Islamic rulers. Even today, there are Christian minorities in states that have been Islamic for centuries. Until the establishment of the state of Israel, there were substantial, important Jewish communities in Islamic states whose ancestors, fleeing from Christian persecution, had been welcomed by Islamic rulers.

The equestrian armies of the Arabic world were, nevertheless, as unsuccessful as their Central Asian counterparts when it came to establishing the stable political and judicial systems necessary for sustainable economic growth. Possibly the orthodox interpretations of Islam's economic and political rules posed a greater obstacle to economic development than those of Christianity. There was also no tension of the kind that existed between the pope and the emperor and between spiritual and temporal power, which had led to the creation of the political and economic freedoms in parts of Europe that underlay the economic upturn there. In any case, the Islamic Empire lost its political and religious unity and broke into provincial states, governed only weakly by the Caliphs in Baghdad. Consequently, the Mongols conquered much of the Islamic world, and in 1258 they also conquered Baghdad. The Islamic world survived the Mongol invasion, but it never regained political unity, just as the Christian world failed to do after the fall of the Roman Empire.

In the long period from the building of the first fortified cities about 8000 BC to the end of the Middle Ages, there was an uneasy balance between fortification technology on the one hand, with which cities and small political units could defend themselves, and siege warfare and transport capacities on the other. In fortified cities and castles, a few people could defend themselves against much larger forces. A successful siege was normally difficult to achieve, requiring not just a superior military force on site but also effective means of transportation. Infrastructures for land transport were particularly expensive to build and maintain. Sea transport, though less expensive, was dependent on wind, weather, and good harbors. Up to the end of the Middle Ages, the use of horses for military purposes probably had the greatest impact on the size of states. During this period, however, it was easier to conquer than to govern. A military advantage that helped carve out an empire had little role to play in transforming such an empire into a politically stable, economically successful state, which would last for centuries. Until the end of the Middle Ages, the Egyptians, Romans, and Chinese were successful but few others were.

This era that had lasted over nine millennia finally came to an end around the year 1500. In 1453, Turkish artillery destroyed the city walls of Constantinople and transformed military technology more radically than the horse had ever done. The development of artillery shifted the military balance decisively in favor of the aggressor and thus paved the way for the large state.

The Turks had already displaced the Arabs in key military positions under the Caliphate of Baghdad. They understood early on the significance of artillery, which they therefore developed. In the 15th and 16th centuries, the Turkish Empire expanded rapidly over much of the Islamic world, however, without successfully conquering and unifying all the Islamic states. They also conquered southeastern Europe, which was Christian, and even besieged Vienna at the end of the 16th century and again at the end of the 17th century, though they were unsuccessful on both occasions.

The military significance of artillery was also quickly recognized by the Europeans and an arms race began in which smaller states, even the wealthier Italian city-states, did not last long. The existing large states such as France and the Habsburg Empire soon proved superior. Sweden developed its natural iron ore resources and metallurgical skills towards the end of the 16th century and rapidly became a major political player in Europe. The possibilities of expansion within Europe were, however, clearly limited, and European powers used their military advantage to build colonial empires beyond Europe's borders. The Spanish and the Portuguese were the first, but the English were the most successful. They all benefited from the fact that significant progress had been achieved in shipping and that ships were fitted with artillery and converted into sailing fortresses, which enabled the successful attack on fortified coastal cities from the water. City walls and forts offered increasingly less protection from such assaults, and it grew ever more difficult to defend cities against these well-armed invaders, especially when outnumbered. Artillery thus shifted the balance decisively towards the large, centrally governed states that had sufficient resources to compete in the escalating arms race in artillery.

Soon after the arrival of artillery, another development reinforced the advantage of the large, centrally governed states: industrialization. Before industrialization, smaller states had the economic disadvantage of having fewer raw materials, and thus being more dependent on trade. Larger states, however, had no advantage in terms of production costs. The benefits of industrial production were already recognized in the Roman Empire: long before the industrial age, pottery was mass-produced and transported throughout the Roman world. After the fall of Rome, however, pottery reverted to being a cottage industry for the local market.

Large states, especially colonial empires, had an advantage not only because they possessed almost all the raw materials they needed within their own borders, but also because of their large domestic markets. In these large states, industrial production often began in state-run factories that manufactured luxury items along with weapons. The large domestic markets arose following the abolition of internal tariffs and other trade obstacles and the introduction of standard weights and measures and a single currency. The internal transportation systems in these states were initially focused on canals because transport by water was less expensive than by land. It was not until around 1,800 that the European road system was finally as advanced as the one built by Rome, some 1,300 years before.

As already mentioned, the Turkish Empire could still besiege Vienna in the 17th century, but by the 18th century it lagged behind the Habsburg Empire. Although it was one of the leading powers worldwide at the time when artillery was developed, the Turkish Empire was not in a position to follow with industrial development. This had not only economic but also military effects, because only an industrial state could produce large quantities of high quality weapons at low costs. It soon became clear that the leading industrial states were those in which not the government, but rather the market and private commerce, played the dominant role. The Turkish Empire and the rest of the Islamic world were unable to build a functioning market economy and private sector, despite their geographic and intellectual proximity to Europe. The Turkish Empire soon came to be called "the sick man of the Bosphorus."

Well into the 19th century, it seemed as if industrialization was some sort of Christian privilege. Until the 16th century, China was in many areas as advanced or even much more advanced than the European powers. Around this time, however, China fell behind due to the rapid development of Europe. It was the industrialization of Japan at the end of the 19th century, however, which proved that a non-Christian culture was in a position to industrialize and become a major power. The war of 1905, in which Japan defeated the Russian fleet, was a shock for Russia and Europe.

Like China, Ethiopia, and Thailand, Japan was spared European colonization. There were several reasons for this. Japan was distant from Europe and had none of the natural resources or riches that the European powers desired. By the time Japan had any contact with Europe, it already had a highly developed, well-organized political system and was able for quite some time to protect itself from foreign influence. Only when the United States had integrated the western part of the American continent did it begin to extend its influence across the Pacific to Japan. In 1853, an American fleet under the command of Commodore Matthew Calbraith Perry forced diplomatic and trade relations upon Japan.

The American success led to a radical change in the policy of the Japanese leadership. The new Japanese leaders realized that applying the European and American models of success to Japan could guarantee Japan a position of equal power on the world stage. Young Japanese were sent to Europe and the United States for their education. Japan's apparent mimicry of the West even became the object of European scorn until the crushing defeat of the Russian fleet in 1905. At the beginning of the 20th century, the world was largely divided between the colonial powers; Japan therefore extended its influence at China's expense. Korea and large parts of China fell under Japanese control and remained so until the end of the Second World War.

The First World War was undoubtedly ignited by a series of unfortunate coincidences, but it was probably unavoidable. War was seen generally as a normal tool of politics. The wars of the 19th century had shown that superior technologies, tactics, and strategies ensured swift victories. The Napoleonic wars were the precedent: they showed that it was possible to use general conscription to build a massive army and to supply it in the field. A combination of artillery and cavalry guaranteed rapid territorial gains. The Prussian–Austrian war of 1866 and the German–French war of 1870 brought decisive victories in a very short time at comparatively little cost. The introduction of the railways made supplying massive armies easier than it had been during the Napoleonic wars. Every European power had optimistic battle plans up its sleeve anticipating quick victories. The Russian defeat by the Japanese led to Russian ambitions in the West; the Russians realized that supporting Slavic nationalism in Europe could lead to Russian expansion and that this would be at the cost of the Turkish and Habsburg empires.

But there was a new development in military technology, which was underestimated by military strategists: the machine gun. The infantry suddenly had a relatively cheap, light, and long-range weapon that could be used not just against opposing infantry, but more significantly against their more mobile opponent, the cavalry. For a brief moment in history, defense, not offense, became the best defense. The First World War marked a return to a time when there was no cavalry, and aggressors had to invest in long and costly sieges requiring large quantities of troops and material. When quick victories did not materialize at the beginning of the war, the Habsburg and German empires were besieged by the Western and Russian allied forces. The Turkish Empire, allied with the German and Habsburg empires, was economically and politically too weak to play a decisive role, and at the end of the war the Turkish Empire finally broke apart.

In contrast to the siege of a city or fortress in the Middle Ages, the First World War offered the defenders a wider geographic area and granted the aggressors little mobility, because cavalry was by and large disposed of by the machine gun. Even if the aggressor broke through the lines of defense with the massive use of artillery and infantry, it could not use cavalry to penetrate deep into enemy territory and bring the defender to the point of collapse. The defending army could always set up a second line of defense a few miles further back. The gain in territory was only a few square miles. In the age of fortresses and city-states, such a loss would have meant total defeat, but for a large empire the loss of a few square miles meant little. The German and Habsburg empires were victorious on the Eastern front and the war there effectively ended with the collapse of the Russian monarchy. However, the war was decided on the Western front, when the United States entered the war and poured in large amounts of fresh troops, arms, and supplies.

During long wars, new weapons, technologies, tactics, and strategies are always developed, and are applied towards the end of the war. Although their significance is mainly lost at the beginning, they are decisive for the next war. Tanks and airplanes, for instance, were used towards the end of the First World War but had little influence on the course of events. This would change dramatically in the Second World War.

The military and political leadership in Germany recognized the importance of these new weapons earlier than others and realized that the new technologies would fundamentally alter the art of war strategically and tactically. When the Nazis seized power, their first priority was to build up a new army.

At the beginning of the war, the Third Reich's opponents had more tanks and airplanes, but strategically and tactically they were stuck in a First World War mindset. In just twenty years, the balance had shifted decisively once again in favor of the aggressor. Long defensive lines with trenches were no longer required; mobile tank formations with high fire power were able either to break through or to avoid them altogether. Machine guns were able to stop cavalry but not a tank formation. The Third Reich's mechanized armies were able to take huge territories even faster than the cavalries of a bygone era.

The Third Reich, however, was no more successful than the equestrian armies of the past in establishing a politically stable, economically thriving political system in its conquered territories. Hitler's forecast "Thousand Year Reich" was finished after just five years of war. Impressive as the military successes of Hitler, Napoleon, Genghis Khan, and Attila may seem, when all is said and done they offered little more to human history than short and bloody episodes, when compared to the long periods of the Roman and later the Holy Roman empires.

During the Second World War, new developments in weaponry again shifted the balance in favor of the defender. Anti-tank weapons, the so-called "Panzerfaust" or "bazooka", were developed for the infantry and inflicted heavy losses on tank units, especially in terrain that offered infantry concealment such as urban areas and forests. The battle of Berlin, for instance, saw weak infantry forces inflicting heavy losses on Soviet tank divisions.

The success of the bazooka at the end of the Second World War led to the development of anti-aircraft missiles for infantry. Although anti-aircraft missiles were only effective against low-flying aircraft or helicopters, they granted infantry significant protection against air attacks in favorable terrain. Anti-tank and anti-aircraft missiles were substantially cheaper to produce than tanks, airplanes, and helicopters, both with regard to production and the training needed to use such weapons.

By the time of the Korean War, just five years after the end of the Second World War, mobility on the battlefield was so reduced that it seemed like a return to the static warfare of the First World War. A surprise assault by the communist forces of North Korea, supported by the Soviet Union and China, took nearly all of South Korea. They were, however, quickly repelled by UN forces led by the United States. Both sides then dug into their positions, and neither could make any decisive territorial gains even though UN forces soon controlled the airspace. The border region between the north and the south was mountainous and thus not suited for mechanized units. Eventually, both parties agreed to a ceasefire, and the border between North and South Korea is to this day based on the ceasefire line.

In the two Vietnam wars, first the French and then the Americans suffered crippling defeats by a well-equipped and trained infantry army, which was both tactically and strategically very well organized. The terrain provided ample cover and concealment for their forces, and, perhaps more importantly, they were willing to take heavy losses. Air supremacy and tanks were useless against infantry under such conditions and in such terrain. The Soviet experience in Afghanistan was much the same.

The wars after 1945 show that aggressors using mechanized formations can only achieve major gains in territory and quick victories in the appropriate terrain and against an opponent who has similarly built his defense upon mechanized formations and an air force. As a general rule, whoever achieves air supremacy at the beginning of such a war wins. Mechanized units with their supply lines are easy targets in open terrain for aircraft even from a relatively high altitude. The wars between Israel and its Arab neighbor states as well as both Iraq wars are good examples of the importance of this.

However, if the opponent has a well-equipped and modern infantry and is prepared to defend cities and terrain that is less suited to mechanized formations, no quick victory can be gained with tanks, absolute air supremacy, and extensive use of helicopters. On the contrary, the chances are high that the heavily armed aggressors will not win. Such a defense strategy is, however, sustainable only under the following conditions:

1. Anyone who is willing to use infantry to defend cities has to be ready to sustain very heavy civilian casualties and large-scale destruction. The only way out of this is either to have a strong civil defense, such as the Swiss have, or to evacuate cities prior to military engagement.

2. Defending a city with infantry where there is still a civilian population requires their support and cooperation; otherwise, there is nothing to prevent civilians from acting as informants for the aggressor.

3. The aggressor has to respect human rights in its treatment of the civilian population. If, however, an aggressor is comfortable with using weapons

of mass destruction, he will take the city or the most difficult terrain. Saddam Hussein, for instance, was willing to use chemical weapons against the Kurds, soldiers, and civilians alike.

It is always difficult to foretell how new forms of military technologies, strategies, tactics, and means of transport will impact on warfare and the size of states in the future. It is easier to form a general idea of where such innovations are most likely to occur. When, for example, the horse started to gain a key role for military purposes several thousand years ago, the people of the steppes were in a favorable position. There, large numbers of horses could be bred and used generally by the population as transport and working animals. From the steppes of Asia and the Arabian peninsula, armies of cavalry rose that were in a position to conquer large areas in a short time because they were superior to the military formations of the agrarian states and empires. With the emergence of artillery, those regions with the necessary natural resources and metallurgical skill had the advantage. Industrialization was the further prerequisite for mass-producing weapons, and that does not seem likely to change in the foreseeable future.

It is therefore possible to eliminate those regions that lack a broad and highly developed industrial base. The economic collapse of the Soviet Union showed that an efficient market economy is also necessary today. This may surprise some readers, but I believe that from a military standpoint neither China nor India can compete with the United States in the foreseeable future. China and India have the necessary industrial base. They also have nuclear weapons and long-range missiles, but an arms race with the United States would undoubtedly bankrupt them sooner or later, just as it did the Soviet Union. To compare defense spending worldwide is difficult, but since the end of the Cold War, the share of the United States is around 50 percent of the total. Britain is next with approximately 5 percent and China follows with somewhere between 4 and 5 percent. The US military research budget, according to some estimates, is greater than that of the next twenty states combined. The private sector also invests far more heavily in research than in China or India. Much of this civilian research, such as in communications and information technology or aircraft design, also has military applications.

The other industrial states such as Japan, Germany, France, and Great Britain are just as unlikely as China or India to pose a threat to US military supremacy during the next few decades. None of these states has a weapons industry that can arm its own troops with cutting edge technologies. The

United States supplies these countries with whole weapon systems, or at least with their most advanced components, which makes their armed forces heavily dependent on the US. They need American satellites for intelligence and reconnaissance, and they need American military transportation to move troops and supplies over long distances. Over the decades, the absolute dominance of the American defense industry has only increased in terms of both quantity and quality, and there is every indication that this trend is bound to continue in the coming decades.

An enthusiastic European may argue that Europe is on its way to creating the United States of Europe and will be America's equal in military power. When the political leaders of Western Europe planned and made attempts to found a European Defense Community after the Second World War, the project was still credible. Western Europe was justifiably afraid that the other military superpower, the Soviet Union, might occupy Western Europe. The Soviet Union had already occupied the whole of Eastern Europe and parts of Central Europe, and had amassed an impressive arsenal of both conventional and nuclear weapons on its western frontier, which left no doubt as to the Soviet capability to annex Western Europe. Western Europe was totally dependent on the military protection of the United States, but the US army was preoccupied first with Korea and then with Vietnam. American assurances to defend Europe if necessary with nuclear weapons were not totally credible in the eyes of many Europeans, because in a nuclear war the United States would have been destroyed too. Nevertheless, efforts to form a European Defense Community failed in 1954. A European Economic Community of six states emerged a few years later as an economic and not a military entity. Its founders hoped that economic cooperation would one day lead to a United States of Europe with a military capacity strong enough to defend itself against possible Soviet aggression without American help. The United States of Europe did not, however, materialize.

Clearly, what could not be achieved under the constant military threat posed by the Cold War will not be achieved today, following the collapse of the Soviet Union. How can the European voter be convinced to take on the enormous financial cost of building Europe into a military superpower, just when no military threat to Europe can be seen on the horizon? Arguably the chief threat today is from terrorism, and a military superpower is no better protected against a terrorist threat than any other state. Even if a United States of Europe is one day possible, its military power will be dwarfed by America's, and this is exactly the way it should be. In the past thousand years, we Europeans have waged more than enough unnecessary wars both in Europe and outside Europe. If there is one thing we should have learned from the past millennium, it is to find a more intelligent goal than becoming a military superpower just so that we can compete in this area worldwide with the United States. Europe has more to offer to the world and should concentrate on working with the United States to make the world a safer, freer, and more prosperous place, as described in Chapter 12.

In the coming decades, humanity will find itself in a fortunate, and from the standpoint of history, quite exceptional, position. For the first time, the world is dominated by one military superpower that has no ambition to expand its territory. American policy can of course be criticized, and mistakes are certainly made from time to time. But a close examination of American military interventions in the 20th century reveals that America never had the intention of conquering territory. In some instances the United States or its allies were attacked; at other times, American leaders believed they had to promote freedom and democracy in one state or another and intervened, sometimes successfully, but all too often not. In all cases, however, the United States eventually withdrew, which was not always what the country it had occupied may have wanted. If the US has a worldwide network of military bases today, it is in agreement with the states in question, with the exception of Guantanamo in Cuba. In the midst of the Cold War, France, for instance, demanded the withdrawal of US and NATO forces, and they quickly complied.

Whoever criticizes the United States today for the Iraq war should not forget that Saddam Hussein was one of the most brutal dictators since Hitler and Stalin. He invaded Iran and Kuwait for their oil fields. He used weapons of mass destruction against Iran and his own population. A more justifiable accusation may be that the United States did not do more during the first Iraq war to bring him down, which would have spared the Iraqi people tremendous suffering. It is clear that little thought was given to developing a sensible plan for building a truly democratic, constitutional state in Iraq. European states, however, were not much more successful with their former colonies in this regard. The failures of the past should therefore be analyzed, and new solutions formulated.

Surprises are, of course, to be expected at a time of radical technological and political change. At the end of the 19th century, no one could have predicted the political revolutions the 20th century would bring. The rise of an aggressive military superpower, while improbable, cannot be ruled out. Technological breakthroughs and political cataclysms could bring about another superpower, unlike the United States, without a democratic constitution and a market economy, driven by a desire for military expansion and the subjugation and assimilation of conquered populations. Such a superpower would eventually fall, but in an age with weapons of mass destruction it could take a staggering part of the world's population along with it. The equestrian armies of Central Asia took many lives and depopulated large territories in their conquests, and their weapons were far more primitive than those of today. We now have the opportunity and the need to develop a clear concept of how to build democratic constitutional states and integrate them into the global market economy. Europe squandered the same opportunity at the beginning of the 20th century, when it governed most of the world. Instead, it caused two world wars. In the 21st century, we may hope that Europeans can work with the United States and other democratic constitutional states and succeed where we failed miserably a hundred years ago.

5. Monarchy, oligarchy, democracy

History shows that it is not easy to develop and implement concepts for states, based on democracy and the rule of law, which will guarantee political stability and economic success. The larger the state, the more difficult the task. There have been many military leaders who were able to conquer large territories in a short time, but only a few succeeded in turning those conquests into lasting states that offered their population the rule of law, prosperity, and freedom. Only those states that had the active or at least the passive support of the population were successful over long periods of time. In the past this could be achieved by religion; today one needs democracy.

In the 19th and 20th centuries, attempts were made again and again to introduce European and American models of democracy both inside and outside Europe. Unfortunately, nearly all of them failed. It therefore makes sense to study the types of state of the past before new types based on democracy are developed and implemented. I have found it rather helpful to rely on the ancient Greeks, who considered the different types of states—monarchy, oligarchy, democracy, and anarchy—as a cycle. The goal is to avoid anarchy and to build a stable state based on the rule of law from the different elements of monarchy, oligarchy, and democracy. Ideally all three elements should be brought together so that they operate in harmony for the benefit of the state and its population.

As mentioned before, elements of monarchy, oligarchy, and democracy can be found in Stone Age hunter-gatherer societies, which have partly survived into our time. For hundreds of thousands of years, people have had to live and solve all kinds of tasks together in order to survive. To kill large and dangerous animals like elephants, rhinoceros, lions, and tigers, people had to work together in large groups over long periods of time with clear command and organizational structures. New and well-preserved archeological evidence shows that the predecessor of modern man, so-called *homo erectus*—who existed in Africa two million years ago and later settled in Europe and Asia—was able to hunt and kill large and dangerous animals and that his life was probably not very different from that of Neanderthal man or the modern man of the Stone Age.

The hunting of large and dangerous animals had to be planned very carefully, from the manufacture of the necessary weapons, through the training of hunters in the use of these weapons, to the development of strategies on how to kill as many animals as possible with a minimum of risk. Careful planning was also necessary to decide what to do once the animals had been killed. Tools had to be ready to cut up and preserve the meat for a time when there was less to eat, such as in winter. For example, evidence has been found at Schöningen in Germany that a large group of *homo erectus* killed a herd of at least twenty wild horses 400,000 years ago. The bodies of the animals were cut up with stone tools and even the bones were used. The archeological evidence shows that *homo erectus* was able to keep all predators away until everything was secured. Either they were able to work very rapidly, indicating that many people were involved, or they were able to set up watches to keep away predators day and night. During these excavations wooden spears were found that are not much different in their aerodynamic properties from the javelins which are used today in competitions. Tests using copies of these spears have shown that they could be used to kill large animals at a distance of twenty to thirty meters.

To be successful in such big game hunting, *homo erectus* had to have an organizational structure and means of communication in the form of language, similar to the hunter-gatherer societies of modern man. Already, then, the group or tribe needed something like a chief or monarch, who was responsible for leading the group. In addition, there must have been smaller groups that needed leadership. Women as well as men were probably involved in the preparation of the hunt, perhaps even took part in it, and certainly played an important role in how the meat was prepared and kept.

If one looks at Stone Age societies that have survived until today, or where there are reliable reports, one sees that at the top of the hierarchy there is a chief and close to him very often a medicine man, who is not only responsible for medicine but also for religious ceremonies. There is also a group of lesser leaders, who have important functions inside the group. The chief as the monarch and the lower chiefs as the oligarchy were only able to fulfill their duties in an efficient way if at least a majority of the group or tribe trusted them. This trust was essential for efficient cooperation and for the survival of the group over generations under difficult and often dangerous conditions. Already in prehistoric times there must have been, besides the elements of monarchy and oligarchy, an element of democracy in these Stone Age groups. Another reason this is likely is the fact that throughout history the element of democracy has usually been stronger in small groups and states than in large ones.

One should not forget, in this context, that the animal kingdom uses similar hierarchies and group structures. There are several animal species, living in groups, that need the cooperation of the different group members and rely on the concept of a leader and an oligarchic structure with subleaders. In recent decades behavioral research has shown amazing parallels between the group behavior of humans on the one hand and different animal species on the other.

The interaction between monarchy, oligarchy, and democracy in small groups of a few hundred individuals is the result of a long evolution. The optimal size of the group has varied, depending on the climate, the geographical environment, and the availability of food. Archeological evidence and surviving hunter-gatherer societies suggest that there were minimum and maximum sizes of population and area. Archeology also indicates trade between groups over large distances. Experience shows that trade between different groups of humans leads to friendships and marriages. Human history was certainly also shaped from its beginning by warlike conflicts over the best resources for food and water, the best residential areas, and the most beautiful women.

Intense competition between the different human groups explains why early Stone Age man settled the whole planet with the exception of Antarctica. In order to survive as a group and to remain independent, the losers in a conflict had to move into new territory and to settle there. One has to be full of admiration for the intellectual achievement of *homo erectus* from tropical Africa. Rather than adapt his body to the environment, as was the case with other species, he adapted his environment to his needs. When our ancestors moved into colder areas, they did not slowly grow thick fur but rather made warm clothes, built huts to protect themselves from the wind and the cold weather, and used fire to warm themselves. When *homo erectus* added larger animals to his diet of fruits and small animals, he did not grow long teeth like the wolf or large claws like the lion, but developed weapons, which he used to kill the largest and most dangerous animals. When he started to live along sea coasts, the shores of lakes, and the banks of rivers, he learned to swim, to build boats, and to make nets, harpoons, fishing rods, and lines in order to catch and eat fish.

The fact that early humans did not physically adapt to the environment, and that there is hardly any genetic difference between people of different regions, is a further indication of the rapid spread of humanity as soon as the genetic conditions were fulfilled for the intellectual development and social structures of the group. Despite all the wars, the genetic exchange between different human groups was intensive. Genetic research shows that neighboring groups of chimpanzees are much less related than different human groups across the continents. Unfortunately, we will probably never know how genetically different *homo erectus* was from modern man.

In any case, *homo erectus* with his intellectual capacities was already highly successful not only as an individual but also in his group structure. In this long and tough competition between different individuals and groups, all those genes and social structures that did not follow the successful model either died out or were wiped out. Whether we like it or not, we are, as individuals and as a social structure, the product of this long selection process.

To give the reader a feeling for the span of human development and selection process from its beginning to our time, I want to use an image which has always helped me to get a feeling for these long time spans. Let us take the time that humans have lived on earth and imagine it as one year. If *homo erectus* two million years ago represents January 1, or the beginning of human development, then only on December 29, 12,000 years ago, did a few people try out agriculture for the first time in a small area. When, on December 31, or 4,000 years ago, agriculture finally spread and started to shape human society, this agrarian-style society was already coming to an end.

Most people today live in a society that has been shaped by the manufacturing and service industries. In a few decades probably only a small percentage of the world population will live as farmers, as is already the case in the more developed regions of Europe, Asia, and North America. Agriculture was never able to shape humanity as much as Stone Age hunter-gatherer societies did, either genetically or with regard to social structure.

Nevertheless, the introduction of agriculture, or what is known as the agricultural revolution, about 12,000 years ago, has influenced the development of the state up to today. This revolution made it possible to feed several hundred thousand people in areas that before were only able to feed a few thousand, provided that the area was appropriate for intensive agriculture and that the population used its knowledge and the appropriate technology. The close cooperation between monarchy, oligarchy, and the people in the relatively small groups of the hunter-gatherer society was replaced by a small group of leaders working with the monarch and the oligarchy on the one hand, and a large population that had to work in the fields on the other.

A population that is dependent on agriculture is much more dependent on storage to feed itself between harvests than a hunter-gatherer society with a low density population in a large area, which usually offers a large variety of food resources all year round. A storage economy and the protection of storage facilities against hungry neighbors led, in the first agricultural areas of the Near East, to the development of fortified cities, which were used as centers for administration and trade and where food stocks were stored and protected. The monarchy and the oligarchy were responsible for administration and military protection. In the advanced agrarian civilizations of the Near East, hunting became more and more the privilege of the monarchy and oligarchy, and they also had the military power. The majority of the population, who worked the land, relied for their living on agriculture and thus became more and more dependent on the monarchy and oligarchy. The element of democracy was slowly pushed back and survived only in small states and societies such as the city-states of ancient Greece. In larger states, democracy had no chance. It would not have been possible to bring together the whole population and then to make decisions in assemblies in the traditional way. Anyone who has visited one of these popular assemblies in some of the cantons of Switzerland, where they still survive, knows that this traditional form of democracy has a limit on the number of participants.

As mentioned before, the time span of the agrarian revolution was too short and humanity with its high intelligence too successful for the revolution to result in a genetic change. However, the social structures in the group and in the states adapted to the new situation. In the larger and usually more successful states, the democratic legitimation of the monarchy and oligarchy disappeared. A new legitimation had to evolve for the state to survive: religious legitimation. In this state structure the monarchy or the monarch was the centerpiece. The monarch was chosen by God or the gods, and acquired divine status, in the large and old empires of Egypt, China, and Japan and the Indian civilizations of Middle and South America. It is interesting to note that in all these different civilizations, the same state model was successful: hereditary monarchy with a strong religious legitimation.

Obviously, this model offered advantages that other models did not. Hereditary monarchies were politically more stable. The clear succession line reduced the battles for power and civil wars, which was much more important in an agrarian economy than in an economy shaped by hunter-gatherers. Destroyed harvests or stolen food stocks brought starvation for large parts of the population. In the hunter-gatherer civilization there are no fields where the harvest can be destroyed. The larger the state, the better the protection for its fields and food stocks against robbery, and the stronger the position of the monarch and the oligarchy became. If such a state succeeded in integrating all the land suited for agriculture in the whole region, the state was protected for a long time from attacking, hunter-gatherer neighbors. Egypt and China are good examples of successful states: once united, empires with a divine monarch at the top remained surprisingly stable over thousands of years. If one dynasty died out or was overthrown, a period of civil war or anarchy might ensue, but those states or empires soon returned to the old model.

The large agrarian states had another advantage compared to neighboring states based on a hunter-gatherer economy or compared to states with an economy based on cattle breeding. In an agrarian economy there is a relatively short and labor-intensive period during cultivation and harvest, and then longer periods where there is not much work to do and where most of this work is rather light and can be done by women. Thus a large agrarian state had a large unused work potential at the disposal of the political leadership. It could be used for military purposes, but this had two disadvantages: first, the soldiers had to be sent back home for cultivation and harvest, and second, the entire male population would have weapons and would be militarily trained. For a political leadership that was not fully supported by the population, this could be a threat. Very often, therefore, agrarian-based states preferred to rely on a professional army and to use the workforce potential instead for building military fortifications, roads, irrigation systems, flood protection, temples, palaces, pyramids, and many other things.

Monarchies had to rely on oligarchic structures to rule over large agrarian states and to fulfill the requisite tasks: military defense, the administration of the storage system, transport and irrigation systems, and—of vital importance in a rule based on religious legitimation—religious administration, with its priests and temples.

Whereas in the hunter-gatherer society there was primarily a division of labor between men and women, in agrarian societies a multifaceted division of labor and specialization developed. This specialization, however, only took place in large states. The geographical limitations of smaller political units, whether they were mountainous or on islands, meant that humans could not specialize to that extent but had to undertake a wide variety of functions. In the developing cities of the larger states there was, on the other hand, a variety of craftsmen, tradesmen, and other professions.

In order to finance the administration, the military, priests, churches, and so on, these states were obliged to impose taxes. Very early in the development of states, taxation was used not only to finance work and tasks for the common good, but to enable monarchs and oligarchs to live in great luxury compared to the farming population. Taxation and the waste of the taxpayers' money is certainly another negative consequence of the agrarian revolution.

In the context of religious legitimation, the oligarchy was normally more or less dependent on the monarch, who could select, nominate, and also dismiss its members. Whenever the oligarchy was able to strengthen its position compared to the monarch, a hereditary oligarchy or nobility emerged and was able to pass on to its children the titles, functions, and economic advantages connected with these positions. This weakened the position of the monarch. Even in states without hereditary nobility, the oligarchy always tried to strengthen its influence to the detriment of the monarchy. This latent conflict between the monarchy and the oligarchy can be seen in different periods and in different regions of the world. Nevertheless, they were dependent on each other and had to live in a symbiosis. The monarch needed the oligarchy to administer and defend the state; the oligarchy needed the monarchy as a religiously legitimated symbol for the people and as an arbitrator in conflicts between the different oligarchs.

Until the American Revolution at the end of the 18th century, few large states had existed that were not hereditary monarchies over long periods of time. Rome prior to the imperial era was an exception. Indeed, during the time of the Roman Republic, internal conflicts and civil wars resulted in the republic becoming a monarchy. The rise of the small Roman Republic to become one of the largest and most important empires in history was possible in part because of the political and geographical fragmentation of Italy, and also because the rapid rise and fall of Alexander the Great's empire left a political and military vacuum in the Mediterranean region. This was initially exploited in the western part of the region by another republic, namely Carthage.

The wars between Carthage and Rome, which lasted for approximately one hundred years, were characterized on both sides by political leadership that was divided and hesitant. The oligarchy of patrician and noble families was often more afraid of a strong and victorious military leader who might take over all political power than it was afraid of the enemy. When Hannibal stood before the gates of Rome, the Roman Republic would have been lost had Hannibal received full support and necessary supplies from the political leadership in Carthage. The retreat of Hannibal and the defeat of Carthage made it possible for the Roman Republic first to gain control of the western Mediterranean and the bordering areas up to the Atlantic coast, and then to conquer the successor states of Alexander the Great's empire in the eastern Mediterranean.

The rise of Rome as the superpower of its time was not the work of an outstanding military leader or of a dynasty which tried over generations to realize the vision of a world empire. It was a long, painful road full of defeats, internal unrest, and civil wars. Rome did not become a world empire by intent or as a result of a long-term strategy, but by the accidents and coincidences of history. When the last Roman king, Tarquinius Superbus, was driven out of Rome in 509 BC, the noble families not only decided to establish a republic under their rule, but also worked out elaborate regulations to prevent, first, a hereditary monarchy, and second, the outbreak of a civil war. In the event the elaborate regulations were not able to prevent either monarchy or civil war, but the political structures and laws provided the foundation for the leading empire of its time. These gave the republican and then the imperial state both the stability to survive all the storms and sufficient flexibility to integrate politically large areas and their populations into the growing Roman Empire. The senate became the dominant political force in the republic, but at times of crisis individual consuls or dictators were granted extraordinary political power for a short time. The other republican city-states of the Mediterranean were less successful and were integrated into the Roman Empire.

The political structures and the laws of the Roman Republic not only provided a solid base for later imperial rule, during which the state model could be further developed, but has also influenced the development of the rule of law in Europe, and from there throughout the world. The study of Roman law was an obligatory part of the training of lawyers well into the 20th century.

The Roman Republic was the most successful republic in human history until it became a hereditary monarchy. Later, other republics emerged which were ruled by oligarchies, such as Venice at the end of the Middle Ages, but none had the size and importance of Rome. It was only two thousand years later, with a new concept of the state, that the United States of America succeeded in becoming the leading world power.

Human history from the beginning of the agrarian revolution until the American Revolution at the end of the 18th century shows that, at least in larger states, a combination of a hereditary monarchy with religious legitimation and an oligarchy was usually more successful than other models. There were different ways to become a member of the oligarchy. If the monarchy was strong, the monarch decided who would become a member of the oligarchy; if the oligarchy was strong, other methods decided on its membership: elections, casting lots, wealth, military achievements, education, or membership of certain families or classes of the population. A strong oligarchy was able to reduce the monarchy to a religious symbol, as was the case in Japan between 1615 and 1868. In that period political power rested not with the emperor, but with a kind of hereditary prime minister, the so-called shogun from the noble family of the Tokugawas.

The state model of a symbiosis between hereditary monarchy and oligarchy turned out to be a success story not only in the agrarian areas of the world, but also in the large grazing areas of Asia and Africa. There, cattle breeding allowed a much higher population density than hunting and gathering. The population with its livestock was far more mobile than the population in the agrarian areas, and led a nomadic life similar to the hunter-gatherers. It was more difficult to unite them under one leadership than the population in agrarian areas, and they were not able to develop the different professional groups or specialized oligarchic structures. On the other hand, all men were potential warriors. For the large agrarian empires, this was no problem as long as those nomadic tribes did not have horses. However, as the horse became a more important element of warfare, the nomadic tribes gained a double advantage. Cavalry was much more mobile than infantry, and therefore made it possible to control larger areas. The smaller population density of the nomadic empires was outweighed by the fact that the nomadic population was used to horse riding and weapons from childhood, whereas the agrarian population was generally less suited for warfare. China, in particular, became a victim of these large armies of horsemen, but so did other parts of Asia, Europe, and North Africa. Over long periods of time, however, military success could not be turned into political success. The victorious armies of horsemen with their nomadic culture had the choice either to retreat or to adapt to the existing political structures and be fully integrated into the much larger population of the agrarian culture after a few generations.

Over hundreds of thousands of years, the symbiosis of monarchy, oligarchy, and democracy had shaped the human population in the small states of hunter-gatherer societies. The agrarian revolution and cattle breeding reduced this symbiosis to one of a hereditary monarchy with religious legitimation and oligarchic structures in most parts of the world. The agrarian revolution made it possible to feed many more people in areas that were suited for agriculture, but the people had to pay a price with their health: deficiencies caused by an unbalanced diet, wear and tear to the body through unnatural work, parasites, and epidemics because of the dense population, especially in cities.

Politically, the agrarian revolution offered the population advantages and disadvantages. In the large agrarian states, it was better protected against attacks and robbery from its neighbors. The state offered some legal protection that facilitated trade both inside the state and with other states. This was necessary for the development of an economy based on the division of labor that could specialize in agricultural produce, cattle breeding, mining, and handicrafts, a development that increased the prosperity of the state and its population.

The political disadvantages of this symbiosis between monarchy and oligarchy for the large majority of the population were also obvious. The larger the state, the fewer the political rights of the population. This creeping erosion of democratic rights often spread to smaller states. Only in remote regions— in the mountains or on islands—or in nomadic tribes was this erosion of democracy less pronounced. Through the loss of political rights, high taxation, or wars, the agrarian part of the population slowly entered into a kind of serfdom or slavery.

The deteriorating living conditions of the agrarian population increased the pressure on people to become part of the oligarchy. Conversely, the existing oligarchs tried to exclude new members and to secure for themselves and their descendants membership of the oligarchy by all means. Monarchy and oligarchy were usually financed through taxpayers' money and very often they did not have to pay taxes and duties themselves. Farmers had to carry a rising tax burden, whereas it was then, as now, easier for merchants and craftsmen to escape taxation or to pass on the tax burden to their customers.

Wars or crop failures could lead to peasant revolts, which failed most of the time, but even when they were successful did not change the system. The monarch and the oligarchy were exchanged, taxes and expenses might be reduced as well as the number of the oligarchs, but then the whole cycle started again. The long history of China or the Roman Empire gives us several examples of this. There are historians who believe that high taxation hastened the collapse of the Roman Empire. The oligarchy paid hardly any taxes; the peasants and other groups who were important for the economy had to carry a high tax burden, with the result that the economy of the empire became weaker and weaker and the defense budget smaller and smaller. At the end of the imperial period, the Roman army was mainly a mercenary force, reluctant to fight without being paid. Serfs and slaves were not suited for military defense, either by training or motivation. The collapse of the western part of the Roman Empire did not lead to a change of system but brought anarchy, and several centuries later the Holy Roman Empire emerged with Emperor Charles the Great.

The model of a symbiosis between a monarchy based on religious legitimation and an oligarchy started to fade when the religious legitimation of monarchy was brought into question and when the possibility emerged that democratic legitimation could be possible even in large states. The successful example of the American Revolution started a worldwide process that even today, after two hundred years, is not yet concluded.

Unlike the American Revolution, the French Revolution with its mass executions was a shock. Nevertheless, it was not possible to turn back the wheel of history in Europe and in the world, even after the failure of the French Revolution and the restoration of the monarchy. During the 19th and 20th centuries, oligarchies with democratic legitimation slowly gained the upper hand in politics through general elections. Sometimes this was a peaceful process, and sometimes a revolution. The economic foundations of the old oligarchy were usually agricultural and forest estates that lost their importance as a result of industrialization. The old oligarchies were noble families closely connected with the monarchy, who, like the monarch, were not happy with democratic legitimation through elections. Since revolutions normally end in a bloodbath, it was in most cases more advantageous to agree on a peaceful compromise solution. Great Britain was a good example and a model for other states: the once powerful House of Lords, which was controlled by the nobility, and the monarchy, had to give up one right after another to the democratically legitimized House of Commons.

The position of most hereditary monarchies was too weak to risk a political battle with an oligarchy with democratic legitimation. The costs of the monarchy were usually financed by taxpayers. Step by step, parliaments had gained control over taxation and the budget and could therefore put pressure on the monarchy. The monarch could not address the people directly and bypass parliament, as the constitutions of the European states, with the exception of Switzerland and Liechtenstein, are based on indirect or very weak forms of direct democracy. To avoid a conflict that was difficult to win, the monarchies, like the old oligarchies, had to retreat step by step.

Insofar as the monarchies were not abolished, their power was drastically reduced, either through changes to the constitution or through the application of the Japanese solution from the time of the Tokugawas. For the people and the outside world the monarch was, according to the constitution, still a powerful man or woman, but internally the monarch had little to say. The signature of the monarch under a law or a change in the constitution became a pure formality from which the monarch could not escape. If the monarch for reasons of conscience was not willing to sign a law, like the late Baudouin, King of the Belgians (reigned 1951–93), the solution was to declare him incapable for one day and have somebody else sign the law. Speeches for the opening of parliament are no longer written by the monarch but by the government, and the monarch merely reads them out.

Since the monarchy still has a symbolic value for parts of the population, this solution is also advantageous for an oligarchy with democratic legitimation. I doubt that this kind of solution makes sense for the monarch and his family. Usually not only has the monarch lost his political power, but he and his family have also gradually lost their freedom of speech. In a number of monarchies, the monarch and members of his or her family have to ask permission from the government or parliament if they want to marry. Toward the end of the 20th century, a new and less enjoyable task was added: the private life of the monarch and his family became the object of general entertainment for the public and the media. Employees and friends of the monarch were bribed and paid to obtain information, photos, or family letters in the hope of increasing the circulation of a newspaper or the number of viewers for a TV station. Those monarchs and their families are not privileged any more, but are sitting in a cage that everybody can look into, and they have no privacy and no freedom of speech or opinion. Under such conditions it is difficult to lead a normal family life and to raise children. For people who have lived in freedom before and marry into one of these families, it is especially difficult to get used to such a life. The task of the monarch and his or her family in these states has been reduced to representational work. They are well paid, but as a normal citizen I would not like to change places with them.

Would it not be more humane to abolish those monarchies, to open the cage, and to give back to the monarchs and their families their privacy and freedom of speech and opinion? Perhaps it would make more sense to keep those monarchies, to respect their privacy, and to give them a political function together with democratic legitimation, as in the Principality of Liechtenstein. The republicans among us should take note that during human history republican periods have been relatively short and periods of the hereditary monarchies relatively long.

6. The American Revolution and indirect democracy

Until the 18th century, the development of states around the world was very much influenced by Europe. The success of the American Revolution in 1776, however, changed this trend, and in the 19th and 20th centuries European countries looked increasingly to the American constitution of 1787 as their model. Latin America and later other continents followed suit. The United States became an inspiring example. The development of this state from its beginnings as an English colony to its status as a superpower is certainly worth closer examination.

Britain's colonies in North America were not just oriented towards England; their European heritage was far more diverse than in other colonies. Spanish, French, and Portuguese colonies, like other British colonies around the world, were inhabited mainly by the occupying colonial power and the indigenous population. Such was the case in the European colonies of Latin America, Africa, and Asia, whereas in North America Britain's colonies mirrored Europe's religious and national diversity. Part of the population had fled from Europe because of their religion: Protestants were fleeing from Catholics, Catholics from Protestants, and other religious minorities from both. If it had not been for a mismanaged conflict over taxes that led to the war of independence, the region of the world that is today the United States would probably have remained a part of the British Empire until well into the 20th century, just as so many other British colonies did.

When the United States achieved independence, the founding fathers faced a problem. Religious diversity made religious legitimation of governmental power hardly possible. Besides, as the former colonies had just rejected the British monarchy, it made little sense now to legitimize a new dynasty. Ideological legitimations like nationalism and socialism had not yet been conceived. In the absence of any other alternatives, democracy was the only way to legitimize the authority of the state. The authors of the American constitution knew from their study of history that traditional democracy had certain limits. Rule by the people required people to assemble. This could only be done within small political units in which voters could easily meet and vote regularly. However, at the end of the 18th century, the United States was already far too large both in area and number of inhabitants for such a model to work. In addition, the founding fathers were afraid that the masses of the people could be easily swayed by populist slogans and endanger not only the rule of law but the very existence of the new state.

The separation of powers in Great Britain was quite progressive for its time and for this reason, despite the grievances over high taxes, the British monarchy served as a model for the American constitution. Over the centuries, the English political system had developed—relatively undisturbed from the outside—a politically stable state under the rule of law on the British Isles, which provides a certain legal security. At the same time, it is important to remember that the British political system of the 21st century is different from that of the 18th. The American system, with a strong president and two equally powerful chambers of congress, namely the Senate and the House of Representatives, is therefore more similar to the British model of the 18th century than to Britain's political system today.

The founding fathers of the United States of America found a solution that was both simple and brilliant. They based their constitution on the English political system, with some improvements, and replaced the religious legitimation of the king with the democratic legitimation of the president. The House of Lords and the House of Commons were replaced with the Senate and the House of Representatives, both elected by the people. Members of the Senate were elected indirectly by the people through state legislatures until 1913 when they, like members of the House, were also chosen directly by popular vote. Other important new developments included a very influential, independent justice system and a high degree of autonomy for individual states. The Supreme Court is a constitutional court in function if not in name: it has the power to annul laws and decrees passed by the president and Congress if they are not in accordance with the constitution. The judges of the Supreme Court are appointed by the president with approval of the Senate and are lifetime positions. Some other judges in the United States are elected directly by the people. Initially the federal states were nearly independent. The Civil War in the 19th century, the two world wars in the 20th century, and an increasing centralization of power in the federal government in Washington over the past few decades have greatly weakened the autonomy of the states. Nevertheless, the American federal states usually enjoy a greater autonomy than equivalent regions in European states, with the possible exception of Switzerland.

History shows that even strongly decentralized nations will, over the course of time, become more centralized and more bureaucratic. Wars often accelerate this process decisively. The so-called Holy Roman Empire was for over a thousand years more the exception that proves the rule. Some claim, however, that it was neither Holy nor Roman and certainly not an Empire.

Another new development in the American constitution was the clear separation of church and state, as well as the commitment to religious freedom. As mentioned before, religious diversity prevented the religious legitimation of the state. Although the founders were, as far as we know, devout Christians, they were philosophically consistent and the foundations for the equality of all religions were laid in the constitution. Freedom of religion did not mean freedom from religion, but freedom for religions with the assurance that the state would not support one religion and oppress another. In the United States today the various religions are in competition with one another, and it is up to every member of a religious group to give his support to his religion as well as to his brothers and sisters in faith. Perhaps this is the reason for America's greater religiosity when compared to Europe.

The founders of the United States of America did not agree on whether their political system was really a democracy in the classical sense. My belief is that neither the American constitution, nor almost any other modern constitution I know of, can be called truly democratic. At the most, one can speak of certain democratic rights. I shall try to justify this claim below.

In all indirect or representative democracies, the people's democratic rights are restricted to personnel decisions. Candidates from various political parties are usually elected as the people's representatives in local, regional, or national offices. Any executive who has to make personal and commercial decisions for a company knows that personal decisions are usually more difficult than commercial decisions, particularly when an unknown candidate from outside is recruited for a management position. The effects of commercial decisions, like opening or closing a factory, or increasing or lowering a price can be calculated and evaluated more easily than the chances of success for a new member of management. In a company, at least, there is the possibility of having personal conversations with the candidates, as well as applying other selection methods. Such options usually do not exist for voters. It may be argued that voters are not choosing a person they do not know, but rather a political program to which the candidate is committed. The programs of modern political parties, however, differ little from one another and are often more similar to car advertisements. Even then, a car buyer has the legal right to sue the car company if the technical claims in a car advertisement are not fulfilled; the disappointed voter, on the other hand, has no choice but to wait a few years and vote for another party. Anyone who defends indirect democracy on the basis of the credibility of party programs puts the credibility of indirect democracy in question.

To limit the democratic principle to indirect democracy perhaps made sense when large parts of the population had little education and illiteracy was widespread. Today, it is much more difficult to justify. First, there is little difference in the level of education between the rulers and the ruled. Even where there are great differences in the level of education within the population, as in a number of African states, one does not gain the impression that the most literate and educated people are in the ruling positions. Second, the whole population has to bear the consequences of bad decisions at the highest level.

The American constitution originally offered a very limited democracy for another reason: it was essentially the democracy of white man. Slaves, women, and the native Indian population, to the extent that it survived, were excluded from democratic rights for a long time. It must of course be recognized that the Greek model for democracy also denied women and slaves democratic rights. Yet in spite of the bloodiest civil war of the 19th century over issues that included the abolition of slavery, the United States and its constitution survived.

Despite its weaknesses, the model of democratic legitimation of oligarchy and monarchy realized by the American Revolution represented a tremendous step forward in the history of the development of the state. For the first time since the agricultural revolution over 12,000 years before, it was again possible to direct the development of the state towards democracy in a large agrarian state. It is fortunate for human history, which has been so amply beset by mistakes and tragedies, that the first constitutional draft for a democratic state based on the rule of law was so successful, in spite of a series of weak points in this constitution.

7. The Swiss constitution of 1848 and the path to direct democracy

Switzerland made a very important step in the direction of more democracy in the year 1848. In some cantons of Switzerland the original form of direct democracy survived as it had been known in ancient Greece. It is true that far into the 20th century women in Switzerland had no voting rights, but unlike the United States and ancient Greece there was no slavery. Before 1848 Switzerland was more a confederation of states than a federal state. Napoleon conquered the old confederation and turned it into a short-lived state. When the Napoleonic Empire collapsed, Switzerland, like the rest of Europe, returned more or less to the old political order.

Nevertheless, the ideas of the French Revolution and the Napoleonic age have shaped Europe and with it Switzerland in a decisive way up to the present time. The restoration of the old order turned out to be unstable. In 1848 political unrest broke out in Switzerland and in other European states. The French Revolution had been aimed against the monarchy, the nobility, the Catholic Church, and the religious legitimation of state authority. Unlike the American Revolution, the French Revolution was unable to create a functioning state order with democratic legitimation, for a number of reasons. To explain them all would be beyond the scope of this book: just a few should be mentioned, however, which might perhaps help to explain why the United States and Switzerland succeeded in forming states with democratic legitimation and why other attempts both within and outside Europe often failed.

The French Revolution tried to replace a religion that was weakened by its close link to the monarchy and the state with the ideology of nationalism. The aim was not the tedious and complicated construction of a decentralized democratic state, with the separation of powers and the rule of law, but a powerful state that would create "heaven on earth" for the French people. In the state with religious legitimation, the good Lord in heaven is responsible for divine justice and for paradise in heaven, whereas in a state based on nationalism the state here on earth is responsible for justice and paradise on earth. The logical conclusion of such a nationalistic concept of the state is socialism. Since the French Revolution, the world has seen more or less unattractive combinations of nationalism and socialism. Sooner or later they have failed, because they were not able to fulfill the hopes of the population; those that have not yet failed will fail sooner or later.

The ideology of nationalism assumed that the state had to care for the welfare of the people and therefore of the nation, which theoretically was not a bad idea. However, the European states of the 18th century were not yet nations and did not have any unified national population. Small, local political units and a division of the population into different classes with different privileges and duties were typical even of the French kingdom, which had followed a policy of unification since the 17th century. This policy of unification met some resistance, but larger economic areas were created that made economic growth and industrialization possible. The abolition of internal duties, a unified currency, the unification of weights and measures, the abolition of private monopolies, and other privileges were in the interest of the consumer and of those producers who were able to adapt and could survive the increased competition.

Quite often the unification of economic areas leads to political problems, especially if not all privileges and monopolies are abolished. There are people who have lost their privileges, and there are producers and employees who have lost their business or their jobs because of increased competition. They try to save their business or their job with all possible means, even extreme ones. There is more at risk for the producer than for the consumer, who can choose between a range of products. Changes in the price and the quality of products occur all the time, and for the consumer it is not always easy to gain an overview and to judge them. In addition, many consumers are convinced that the successful producer is making much money at their expense. They envy him, especially when he shows his wealth in public. The consumer, however, rarely goes into the street to fight for lower prices and better quality. The consequence is that there is little political support from those people who gain the most by the opening of the markets and the creation of large economic areas.

To solve this difficult political problem the political leadership, perhaps correctly, did not trust the wisdom of the people. At the end of the 18th and the beginning of the 19th century, the majority of people were illiterate, and as today only a small percentage of the intellectual elite was interested in or familiar with the laws of a market economy. It was natural to rely on familiar religious symbols and to convince the people that they were "the chosen people." Instead of the good Lord in heaven and a very human monarch by the Grace of God here on earth, the now almighty absolute state would create heaven for "the chosen people" on earth.

The next logical step was that the state should grant to all people what they needed and what they deserved. To reach this goal all means of production had to be nationalized and an all-embracing state bureaucracy was necessary. At the end of human evolution, true socialism would be attained. History has shown that neither nationalism nor socialism can create heaven on earth or even the withering away of the state, as many socialists believed at the beginning. On the contrary, as nationalism leads to socialism, so socialism leads to the almighty bureaucratic state, perhaps with the small difference that there is no "chosen people" but a "chosen class of the workers and farmers." When analyzed in greater detail, it is clear that a nationalistic and socialistic policy, which still has many supporters particularly in the Third World, is in fact extremely non-social and is directed against the national interest.

Switzerland and the United States have escaped this fate up to now because their populations are very diverse, both religiously and nationally. In Switzerland there are four language groups: German, French, Italian, and Rhaeto-Romansch. The Catholics are the largest religious group, but in the 16th century Switzerland was an important center for the Reformation, with Calvin and Zwingli both operating from there. As the borders between the twenty-six cantons were not drawn along linguistic or religious divides, the linguistic or religious majority can change from community to community within a canton.

In Switzerland religious legitimation, if present at all, could not simply be replaced by the ideological legitimation of nationalism. The varied structure of the population and the geographical conditions encouraged the creation of a decentralized democratic state based on the rule of law and separation of powers. Neither the population in the United States nor that of Switzerland wanted to have a powerful central state which would create heaven on earth. They feared that a powerful state would create heaven on earth for a small minority at the expense of a suppressed majority.

A strong centralized state would also have reduced the democratic rights of the voters in the communities and cantons of Switzerland. The development of democracy in Switzerland and the United States was not only a top down process: it was just as much a process from below, developing from the communities upward. The growth of democracy from the smallest political unit, the community, upward is probably critical if a state based on democracy and the rule of law is to remain stable over long periods of time. This assumes, however, that the leadership from above encourages the growth of a state based on democracy and the rule of law. Democracy in the smallest political unit is only viable if the voter also has the right to make financial decisions for this political unit. In a strong centralized state, where the smallest political units are merely the recipient of orders and money, democracy and the rule of law will sooner or later be undermined.

Just as the founding fathers of the United States were able to take advantage of the English experience when they wrote their constitution, so the authors of the Swiss constitution were able to benefit from the century-old experience of direct democracy in their cantons as a confederation of states, as well as the experiences of indirect democracy in Europe and in North and South America up to the middle of the 19th century. For example, if written ballots were successful in indirect democracy, there was no reason not to use them in a direct democracy too.

In a direct democracy the political right of the people is not reduced to the election of a representative, who then makes all the decisions for them; the people themselves have the right to make material decisions. In the Swiss, the Liechtenstein, and other systems which have elements of direct democracy, two fundamental rights can be distinguished:

1. *The referendum, which gives the people the right to vote directly on a decision of parliament.* Once parliament has made a decision, people can collect, within a specified period, a minimum number of signatures from voters demanding that the decision of parliament should go to a popular vote. If a majority votes against the decision of parliament, the law will not come into force. For practical reasons, not even in a direct democracy is it possible to have a referendum on every decision by parliament. The referendum is therefore confined to decisions relating to the constitution and the law. Switzerland also has obligatory referendums for a series of decisions at federal, canton, and community level. The problem with these obligatory popular votes is that people have to vote on subjects of

little interest. This is probably the most important reason for the many popular votes in Switzerland and the low participation of voters, which, of course, calls into question the democratic legitimation of some of those decisions.

2. *The right of initiative.* This allows citizens to put forward initiatives, with a legally determined number of signatures collected within a certain period, proposing a change in the constitution or the law. Parliament can then either accept or reject the proposition. If parliament rejects it, a popular vote is necessary and the people decide for themselves. Parliament also has the right to make a counter-proposal, which can lead to a situation where both proposals are rejected by the people and everything remains as before.

The greatest difference between the United States and Switzerland is in the state structure. In the United States the counter-balance to the oligarchy in Congress and the courts is a strong "monarch" with democratic legitimation, namely the president. In Switzerland the monarch is missing. The executive branch, legislature, and the courts are controlled by an oligarchy with democratic legitimation. The counter-balance in Switzerland to the oligarchy is direct democracy. In both the United States and Switzerland, autonomy at the local state level and the cantons is also, to a certain degree, a counter-balance to the oligarchy of federal institutions. Nevertheless, one has to emphasize that during the 20th century the autonomy of the states in the United States and of the cantons in Switzerland has been severely eroded. The central state and thus the bureaucracy expanded, thus strengthening the oligarchy. The more centralized the state and the more diverse the tasks of the state become, the more difficult it is for a monarch, either elected or not, and the people to oversee and to control the oligarchic bureaucracy which is necessary to fulfill these many tasks. This raises the question of whether this process toward a centralized bureaucratic state, dominated by an oligarchy, can be stopped and reversed in both Switzerland and the United States.

The Swiss model of direct democracy has without doubt brought the people more democracy than the indirect democracy of the United States. Why has the Swiss model not been more successful either inside or outside Europe during the past 150 years? One reason might be that the new oligarchies were mainly interested in replacing the legitimation of the old oligarchies and monarchies and not so much in giving the people more democratic rights. In the name of democracy, the religious and dynastic legitimation of the old monarchies and oligarchies was destroyed. The majority of the people had no idea how democracy worked in reality. In the 18th and 19th centuries, there was a continuous democratic tradition only in Switzerland, in Iceland, and on a local level in some parts of the world. For the new monarchs and oligarchs it was, therefore, easy to describe indirect democracy as the best model for the new age. It had the advantage of giving the new monarchs and oligarchs a democratic legitimation without forcing them to give up too much political power.

Much more could be said about the constitutions and state models of Switzerland, the United States, and other states. I hope the reader will forgive me if, as the Reigning Prince of Liechtenstein, I use the Principality of Liechtenstein as my third example. Despite its small size, Liechtenstein has made an interesting contribution to the development of democracy and to the development of the rule of law. Anyone who has studied the different constitutions of human history will notice that the Liechtenstein constitution contains a number of new elements.

8. Liechtenstein's constitutional reform of 2003

As has already been mentioned, the United States is based on a "monarchy" and oligarchy with democratic legitimation, whereas Switzerland has an oligarchy with democratic legitimation and direct democracy. Liechtenstein has all three: monarchy, oligarchy, and direct democracy. Liechtenstein is the first and only example in constitutional history of a state in which these three elements come together and contribute to a largely harmonious and balanced political system. The main reason is that apart from Switzerland, Liechtenstein is the only state in which direct democracy is fully developed. In other states direct democracy tends to take the form of plebiscites to serve the interests of monarchs and oligarchs, and it does not go as far as in Switzerland and Liechtenstein. The right to call for a popular vote may rest with the monarch or the oligarchs, and even if the people have such a right, the popular vote tends to have a consultative character only.

The first Liechtenstein constitution of 1862 was still influenced by the German Confederation, of which it was a member until the Confederation's dissolution in 1866. The constitution was based on the principles of monarchy and oligarchy, and the judicial system was well developed for its time and for a country of its size. However, Liechtenstein did rely on Austria for its laws and judges.

During the First World War, Liechtenstein remained neutral, but the disintegration of the Habsburg monarchy, with which the Principality and the Princely Family of Liechtenstein had had excellent relations for centuries, had political consequences. Following the war Liechtenstein turned its foreign and economic policies towards Switzerland. The customs treaty with Austria-Hungary was replaced by an agreement with Switzerland. On the domestic front there were calls for more democracy. This led in 1921 to a fundamental reform of the 1862 constitution.

The constitutional state was developed according to the most up-to-date thinking at the time, for instance, with a comprehensive constitutional and administrative judicial system. Following the example of Switzerland, direct democracy was introduced at both state and community level. Of course, it must be kept in mind that local communities had always exercised a relatively large measure of autonomy, just as in Switzerland.

The Swiss experiences of direct democracy were extremely valuable and instructive. Nevertheless, some improvements to the Swiss model were undertaken. No obligatory referendums at state level were written into the constitution, which, as mentioned, force the people to vote on matters of little interest to them. If in Liechtenstein part of the population disagrees with a decision of parliament, 1,000 votes or 5 percent of the voters can demand a referendum within thirty days. The Prince, as the head of state, ratifies a law or a constitutional addendum only after this period of thirty days has expired.

Compared with the Swiss system, Liechtenstein expanded the right of initiative, that is, the right of the people to propose a law or constitutional amendment. In Switzerland only constitutional initiatives are possible at state level, while the people of Liechtenstein have the right to propose both laws and constitutional amendments. Proposing a law requires 1,000 signatures and proposing a constitutional amendment requires 1,500. When a constitutional amendment is proposed in Switzerland, the parliament has years in which to accept or reject the proposal or to offer the people a counter-proposal. From a democratic and constitutional standpoint, this is not entirely unproblematic, because it allows an oligarchy to delay the referendum for years. Liechtenstein found another solution. Whenever the initiative takes place, parliament has to declare its position at its next sitting and has three options:

1. it accepts the initiative, based on whatever majority vote is required by the constitution in such a case;

2. it rejects the proposal without offering a counter-proposal;

3. it rejects the proposal and offers a counter-proposal.

If parliament rejects the proposal, the government is required to hold a plebiscite immediately. Compared to Switzerland, the element of democracy is thus strengthened in Liechtenstein to the detriment of the oligarchy.

The unusual strength of direct democracy in Liechtenstein's constitution is easier to understand in the context of the monarchy's historically strong position. The monarch has the right to veto resolutions from the people or parliament; this power of veto has been exercised in the past and will be exercised in the future if the monarch deems it necessary. The Liechtenstein model thus protects against initiatives that are too populist at the cost of the general good or that would negatively impact on minorities. What Switzerland tries to achieve by postponing a decision of the people over years, Liechtenstein achieves with the Prince's power of veto or simply the threat of veto. The Prince exercises or threatens to exercise his veto only if it is truly called for, so as not to endanger the authority and legitimacy of the monarchy.

In the constitution of 1921, the monarch still possessed a religious and dynastic legitimacy and a very strong position, which he could theoretically have exploited to institute a dictatorship quite legally. This gave small groups who were skeptical or negative toward the monarchy the opportunity to criticize it repeatedly. The critics argued that for reasons of principle a hereditary monarchy cannot be democratically legitimized. They claimed that in our time a monarch can only have a justifiable role if this role is reduced to pure representational work without a political function. To put it less politely, these critics wanted to limit the role of the monarch to that of a "yes man." As a counterargument one can point out that most hereditary monarchies have at least an indirect democratic legitimation and that the position of the monarchy in the constitution in Liechtenstein was ratified by popular vote and a democratically elected parliament. And in any political system, unelected appointees, such as judges and government officials, perform political functions according to the constitution and might make very important decisions, e.g. the judge in a constitutional court.

Critics of the monarchy in Liechtenstein are in a particularly difficult position because the Princes and the Princely House have always successfully upheld the constitution and strengthened the economy. All costs of the monarchy are born by the private estate of the Prince and the Princely House; furthermore, over the centuries the Princes have often subsidized the country and its people with donations from their private estate. Support of this kind was interrupted by the Second World War and its aftermath. Despite Liechtenstein's neutrality, Czechoslovakia confiscated all the assets of Liechtenstein citizens after the war. This was a serious blow, as over 80 percent of my family's estate was in Czechoslovakia. The economic setbacks of the time also weakened the Princely House and the monarchy politically. Initial attempts to rebuild the assets were unsuccessful, and the danger loomed that the monarchy might become financially dependent on taxes and thus on politicians. The costs of the monarchy were essentially financed after the Second World War through loans and the sale of art and real estate.

My father therefore suggested very early to me that I should study economics and business instead of history, archaeology, or physics, which I thought were more interesting. Immediately after I had finished my studies in 1969, I had to reorganize and rebuild the family business. After I had more or less successfully finished this job in 1983, my father entrusted me with the exercise of his sovereign powers in 1984. The Liechtenstein constitution gives the Reigning Prince the possibility of entrusting the heir apparent with the exercise of his sovereign powers as his representative. In the past different princes have taken advantage of this possibility, and I did the same with my eldest son in 2004. Our family believes that the Reigning Prince should not assign this important job to his successor only after he is unable to fulfill it because of his age, but rather when the successor is ready to take it over. Another advantage of this solution is that the Reigning Prince can act as an advisor to his successor.

Although the monarchy's critics were a small, albeit vocal group, we in the Princely House came to the conclusion following the death of my father that we should address their justified concerns. The first step was to reform the internal family house law. Ever since the Middle Ages, the Princely House has had a private house law governing membership, voting rights, and succession within the family. The house law had not been changed since 1606 and was clearly in need of revision. The new house law of 1993 was published in the Liechtenstein law gazette (*Liechtensteinische Gesetzessammlung*) for the first time, in response to the wishes of the people. Apart from the above-mentioned points, the new house law includes a procedure for the Prince's deposition as head of the family and head of state if he loses the confidence of the voting family members by abusing his power or for any other reason.

The next step was a fundamental revision of the constitution. The revision proposed by the Princely House met with considerable resistance from parliament, gaining only thirteen of twenty-five votes. The constitution of 1921 stipulated that constitutional amendments would require a three-quarters majority in parliament or a simple majority in a popular vote. So we turned to the people and collected the necessary signatures, hoping to achieve our goal with a popular vote. Critics of the monarchy did the same, presenting to the people a proposal that would have weakened the monarchy. The referendum of March 16, 2003 was decided in favor of the monarchy: the proposal of the Princely House won 64 percent of the votes, the counterproposal won 16 percent, and 20 percent voted to retain the old constitution.

The constitution of 1921 stipulated that judges be proposed by parliament and appointed by the Prince. Theoretically a good solution, in practice this had led to an appointment process beset by party politics. Appointments of judges became part of coalition agreements. If the majority in parliament changed, the majority and the chairmanship in the highest courts changed too. The Prince had the option either to stand by and watch, in the hope that the courts would function reasonably well, or to risk a conflict with parliament, with the danger that seats in the courts would not be occupied. The parties would then blame the Prince for the dysfunctional courts, a risk the Prince, with very few exceptions, had generally chosen not to take.

Under the new laws, judges' terms of office in the highest courts no longer come to an end simultaneously but are staggered and the judges themselves elect the chair. Candidates for the courts used to be elected at party meetings; now an independent commission chooses candidates and presents them to parliament. This commission includes representatives from the government and parliament and is chaired by the Prince. If the commission and parliament cannot agree on a candidate, the judge is elected by the people in a popular vote.

In the constitutional discussions of the 1990s, however, the central concern was not the competence and independence of the judiciary, but rather the status of the monarchy. In view of the strong position of the monarchy in the constitution, it seemed to us in the Princely House that the constitution's indirect legitimation of a hereditary monarch was insufficient. Opponents of the monarchy might claim that the abolition of the monarchy using the procedures laid down in the constitution of 1921 still needed the monarch's consent. To counter such an objection, we in the Princely House developed a new model in constitutional history, namely, a hereditary monarchy with direct democratic legitimacy.

An article was introduced into the constitution that gives the people of Liechtenstein the right, within the framework of a constitutional initiative, to put forward a motion with 1,500 signatures for a popular vote on the abolition of the monarchy. Should a simple majority vote in favor of abolishing the monarchy, parliament has to draft a new constitution based on a republican model. Ratifying this new constitution would again require a popular vote. In order to exercise its political functions, the monarchy in Liechtenstein therefore always needs the confidence of a majority of voters and thus democratic legitimation.

The new constitution also gave the people the option of separating the monarchy as a form of government from the person of the monarch himself. If the people have shown in a popular vote that they have lost their trust in the monarch, then, according to the constitution and the house law, the Princely House decides whether or not the Prince is to be deposed. There may be situations where the majority of the people have lost their trust in the Prince for good reason, and there may be others where the Prince has lost their trust because he has taken a correct but unpopular decision. In the latter case, the Prince still deserves the trust of the Princely House, and it is up to the people to decide whether then to accept the decision of the Princely House or to abolish the monarchy.

Another new element in constitutional history was also introduced—an article that establishes the wishes of local communities concerning membership in the Principality of Liechtenstein. The right of self-determination has thereby been created at the local community level. There are parallels: a right of secession for individual republics had in fact existed in one of the constitutions of the Soviet Union, thus providing the right of self-determination at the republic level. However, the Soviet constitutions were always quite distant from reality and their primary purpose was propaganda. When the Soviet Union collapsed, this constitution was no longer in force, and the secession of the individual republics was not a democratic, constitutional process.

Democracy and self-determination are closely linked and difficult to separate. Either one believes that the state is a divine entity to be served by the people and whose borders are never to be questioned, or one believes in the principle of democracy and that the state is created by the people to serve the people. If one says "yes" to the principle of democracy, one cannot say "no" to the right of self-determination. A number of states have tried to separate democracy and the right of self-determination, but they have never successfully put forward a credible argument.

The most important argument for such a separation between democracy and self-determination is the claim that self-determination only applies to ethnic groups, and that only an ethnic group has the right to demand statehood. Are the Basques and the Kurds not ethnic groups? Are the Swiss or the Liechtensteiners an ethnic group? The Swiss differ among themselves in terms of language, race, and religion more strongly than they differ from respective groups across the border in Germany, France, or Italy. The same can be said of Liechtensteiners, Austrians, and many others. It is simply the vicissitudes of history that have granted statehood and the right to self-determination to some and denied it to others. How is one to explain this discrepancy to those who are denied this right when it is granted to others?

We in the Princely House are convinced that the Liechtenstein monarchy is a partnership between the people and the Princely House, a partnership that should be voluntary and based on mutual respect. As long as we in the Princely House are convinced that the monarchy can make a positive contribution to the country and its people, that a majority of the people desire this, and that certain conditions are fulfilled, such as the autonomy of our family as established in our house law, we shall gladly provide the head of state. This partnership goes back some three hundred years and it has been successful for both the monarchy and the people. Liechtenstein, as I have mentioned, retained its neutrality in both world wars and has been spared war since the beginning of the 19th century. After the Second World War, a thriving, multifaceted economy has developed which has given the Liechtenstein population one of the highest per capita incomes in the world, in a country with hardly any natural resources.

9. The deficiencies of traditional democracy

Indirect democracy, as enshrined in the American constitution of 1787, which served as a model for most democratic states, is a weak form of democracy if analyzed carefully. Compared to the state with religious legitimation, not much has changed concerning the state structure and the distribution of power inside the state. Political power still lies in the symbiosis of monarchy and oligarchy. Monarchs and oligarchs are elected either directly or indirectly by the people, but for the people it is very difficult to know from the outside where real power and responsibility lie. Does power lie with the president, the prime minister, the leaders of the parties, the financial supporters of the party, the courts, or perhaps after all with parliament, or are the members of parliament only the puppets of the party leaders? As mentioned before, only the character of the legitimation has been changed.

The resistance of the oligarchy to giving more power to the people and to developing direct democracy explains to some degree why the ideologies of nationalism and socialism gained so much ground and why all too often only lip service was paid to democracy, as it had been to religion. Nationalistic and socialistic ideas gained strong influence in the 19th and especially the 20th century. Like religions, they have a strong emotional element. It is much easier to mobilize masses of people with populist slogans and ideologies than to engage them in the long, tedious, and complicated process of creating an efficient democracy and the rule of law. The oligarchies and monarchs in power, whether elected or not, not only have to engage the people and themselves in this process but also have to be willing to give up power. Democracy cannot be built only from the top down but, more importantly, also has to be built from the bottom up, especially in large states. This means delegating political power from the center to small political units, as happened in the United States and Switzerland. Of course, the process there was much easier because the building of the state was started from the bottom up by nearly independent states that then united. Less power at the political center in a democracy means fewer opportunities for those with influence in the state to buy votes one way or the other.

Most voters expect that the state will create heaven here on earth, and governments have often done their best to provide it in the hope of proving popular. So, typically, the welfare state was built up, the army of bureaucrats increased, the tasks that the state took over became more diverse, and the compendium of laws became much larger, more comprehensive, and more complicated. Even in small states, the entire state bureaucracy has thus grown out of control. Neither government nor bureaucracy, let alone parliament, has a complete overview of the whole state administration and how the different parts of the administration work together and, unfortunately, often also against one another. In industrialized states, taxes and duties have grown continuously over recent decades to finance the state administration. Efforts to reduce taxes and duties have usually only been successful for a short time, often leading to higher debt, with the consequence that taxes and duties have to be raised again.

All this is not surprising as long as most politicians and voters are rooted in the ideologies of nationalism and socialism. In most democratic states the parties are divided into right-wing and left-wing parties. The right-wing parties are nationalistic and the left-wing are socialistic. The parties in the middle try to be both. Few people up to now have noticed that, in reality, nationalism and socialism are the obverse and reverse of the same worthless coin, which in the age of globalization is slowly rusting away before our eyes. Nationalism and socialism are the names of a political cul-de-sac, which leads only from right to left and again from left to right, but not ahead into the future. Nationalism and socialism have divided people into nations and classes that are fighting each other. If it is not possible to lead the state into the future in this age of globalization, the state will rust and end up on the trash-heap of history. Globalization, which nationalists and socialists resist so hard, is again leading people back into the large family which genetically it has always been. Globalism is depriving the ideologies of nationalism and socialism of their justification for existence.

Nationalism and socialism have created states with huge bureaucracies and oligarchies that now feel their existence threatened by the rapid progress of globalization. Just as regional economic unification met political resistance in nation-states in the past, so now does the accelerating globalization of the world economy. Yet globalization is resulting in a substantial gain in prosperity for the whole world, just as the unification of the economic regions did for nation-states. The enemies of globalization from right and left try to turn back the wheel of history, without realizing that they are putting in jeopardy the existence of their own states and their own people.

As early as the 18th century, students of the economy realized that free trade within a state and between states was advantageous for everybody involved. That raises the question of why human behavior has not adapted to this fundamental fact. Why was liberalism, which was the consequence of this discovery, not more successful during the 19th century?

One reason might have been the perceived threat to the safety of supply channels. Trade between states works smoothly only in peacetime. Even then, restrictions on exports, the blockage of trade routes, and other events can endanger supply channels. Furthermore, customs duties are an easy way to finance the state and the oligarchy, and can also be used along with other import restrictions to protect parts of the local economy from foreign competition. Influential groups in politics and the economy like to use the fears and ignorance of large parts of the population to their own advantage but to the disadvantage of the state and its people.

Besides the economic advantages for some parts of the economy, restrictions on free trade also protect jobs that might otherwise be lost. The loss of a job hurts not only the person who has lost his job, but also those who are dependent on him. Nevertheless, jobs that add no value for the whole population are a burden for the economy. In an economy that is less developed, low-paying jobs are still attractive and will add to the prosperity of the whole population there. This can lead to increased imports from the higher developed economies and to the creation of new and more valuable jobs in those states that have lost jobs to cheaper labor.

Neither the safety of supply channels nor job security can justify limitations on free trade. As far as vital products are concerned, securing the supply can be achieved more cheaply by using large storage facilities than by making the consumer and the taxpayer pay direct or indirect subsidies for whole branches of the economy. In recent decades economic sanctions against some states have also shown that the supply channel can be sustained until the state's economy adapts to the sanctions. For the majority of the population to accept free trade, it is probably more important that people who are unemployed and want to work have adequate financial support until they can find a new job. All those measures will always be a tightrope walk between benefits that are necessary from a social point of view and benefits that are not conducive to the job search. Over a long period of time, only those states that help their people to benefit from globalization instead of protecting them from globalization will increase the welfare of their population.

Liberalism has used many of these arguments in its political fight for free trade. Unfortunately it has remained a rather small political movement of an intellectual elite, which with the introduction of universal suffrage lost out against the parties of the masses based on nationalism, socialism, and the Christian religion. In 19th-century Europe, the political enemies of liberalism were the conservatives, the farmers, and the craftsmen, who saw free trade as a threat. On the European continent, even large areas of industry were happy to impose protective tariffs against the competition of leading British industries. To attain at least some economic liberalization inside the state, liberal forces on the continent formed an alliance with national forces. Liberal nationalists stood in opposition to conservative religious groups. The Catholic Church, especially, saw liberalism as its main enemy in the 19th century and at the beginning of the 20th century. The Church and liberalism had different views not only on politics and economics, but also on many questions of morality.

Neither in the 19th nor in the 20th century was liberalism able to win the hearts of the people. For churches and religious groups, the continual erosion of the religious legitimation of the state led to a loss of political influence. In Europe nationalism and socialism thus replaced liberalism and the Christian religion as the main political force. The result was two world wars and concentration camps in the 20th century, with millions of people killed.

Christianity and liberalism share many fundamental values. Both place the main emphasis on the individual, with his freedom and his responsibility, and not on the state as in nationalism and socialism. In liberalism the individual is responsible to himself; in Christianity, to God. Liberalism and Christianity, as well as other religions, concern all people: they are catholic in the original sense of the word. Liberalism and Christianity believe that the state has to serve the people and not the other way around. Now, at the beginning of the 21st century, has not a time come for liberalism and Christianity, especially the Catholic Church, to bury the hatchet of the 19th century and work in common for the welfare of humanity in the third millennium? Would it not be a common goal to turn states into service companies for humanity?

If, in the age of economic globalization, ideologies like nationalism and socialism have lost their justification, we might reasonably ask what justification for the nation-state remains. Has not the state been reduced to a service company, which has to offer its customers a more or less decent service for a certain price, namely duties and taxes?

Imagine the people as the shareholders of the state, and elections as shareholders' meetings, where the people either offer or withdraw their support for the management team for another four years. Are not popular votes over state taxes and benefits more or less the same as votes on dividend policy, changes of capital, or other important decisions for the company, which have to be taken by the shareholders according to the company's articles of association?

To compare a modern democratic state in the age of globalization with a company is understandable, but at least in my opinion, the analogy is not accurate. In a company the shareholder can sell his shares if he is not happy with the policy of the management or is outvoted at the shareholders' meeting. With the same money, on the same day, he can buy shares in another company or use the money for something else. A citizen who cannot accept the policy of the government any more and who has been outvoted has to emigrate and accept all the related problems, assuming that another state will accept him. It usually takes years before he is allowed to vote, and during that time the policy in his new state might become just as unacceptable as in the old state.

The citizen is much more at the mercy of the service company state than a shareholder is at the mercy of any private enterprise. The type of company that could be best compared to the state is a private monopoly, which not only lays down the rules but is also both referee and player. Despite the separation of powers in an indirect democracy, the oligarchy controls legislation, the courts, and the government. The people as the small shareholder can then only choose at the shareholders' meeting every four years between a few syndicates—the so-called political parties. The syndicates then negotiate between themselves what the rules of the game will look like, who will become referees, and who is allowed to play. In order not to subject the people to the arbitrariness of a political oligarchy, it is critical to include safety measures in the state of the future, in addition to the separation of powers and indirect democracy.

Monarchy and oligarchy, whether elected or not, form a symbiosis in many states and have to rely on democratic legitimation, either directly or indirectly, if they want to exercise political power. It is understandable that a monarch needs an oligarchy in a larger group and in a larger territory. A monarch cannot make all the decisions, implement those decisions, or check whether they have been realized. Not everything can be written down in regulations and laws. Oligarchic structures, be they of a more formal or informal nature, are therefore necessary. A pure monarchy, either with an elected or a hereditary monarch, would be incapable of acting in a state without an oligarchy.

This is even more true in a pure democracy, because the people cannot come together all the time to debate and vote on all matters. The exercises in grassroots democracy at some universities during the 1960s were very instructive. A few student leaders made the decisions with the support of small groups and all the others had to run behind.

Monarchy and democracy need the oligarchy in a state based on the rule of law. But does the oligarchy need both democracy and monarchy? As history has shown again and again, it does not need democracy as long as it can find a credible alternative to democratic legitimation. History also shows, however, that a pure oligarchy without monarchy and democracy has not been a success story. An oligarchy governing a state tends toward slow and cumbersome decision-making that looks for the lowest common denominator. Under such circumstances a state can easily lose its competitive edge. The old Polish state, which collapsed in 1795, was an oligarchy of noble families and in this respect is often cited as an example.

The oligarchy can make compromises with relative ease in its decision-making at the expense of a third party, especially in a state that is more or less a monopoly. A strong oligarchy will therefore always try to reduce a monarch step by step to a symbolic function or completely abolish the monarchy. However, compromises are made to the detriment of not only the monarch but also the people. Taxes and duties are raised as far as possible to give the oligarchy and its supporters all kinds of advantages. In an economy where there is competition, pure oligarchic leadership structures are usually confined to small banks, auditing companies, or lawyers' offices. In other areas of the economy, the model of pure oligarchic leadership has not been very successful.

The rule of an oligarchy with democratic legitimation in an indirect democracy could be even more problematic than the rule of an oligarchy that does not seek democratic legitimation at all. Even during the old Roman Republic, the oligarchy tried to buy the support of the people with *panem et circenses* (bread and circuses). The United States has the longest and most extensive experience of indirect democracy, and there the "buying of votes" with taxpayers' money or with tax benefits is simply called "pork." Such gifts are expensive, and are funded not out of politicians' own pockets but by taxpayers. Voters are recruited from different groups with different interests. To win an election, politicians and parties have, on the one hand, to satisfy their loyal voters, and on the other, to win the support of floating voters or even the loyal voters of other parties. In order to reach this goal, they make promises that realistically cannot be kept. Moreover, there is a strong temptation not to raise taxes in order to pay for what has been promised to the voters, but first to raise the debt burden, or just print money. As a state can print money and increase debt for quite some time before the voter begins to feel the effects, it is probable that those politicians and parties who were responsible for those policies will no longer be in office when it becomes a problem. The problem must be assumed by other politicians, parties, and governments, which must either make themselves unpopular by introducing drastic measures in the budget or be blamed for the resulting economic chaos and inflation. Since few voters and politicians understand the rather complex inter-relationships in a national economy, especially those of a long-term nature, one cannot really blame them. The problem lies with the system and not the politicians.

The system more or less forces politicians to pursue special interests and not the common interest; otherwise, they run the risk of breaking their election promises and losing the confidence of voters. In addition, it is very difficult for a politician in an indirect democracy to follow a long-term policy that is in the common interest, as his fate and that of his party is decided at the next election.

If one assumes, first, that the oligarchy is by far the strongest element of the three elements of monarchy, oligarchy, and democracy; second, that rule only by the oligarchy sooner or later creates problems; and third, that the oligarchy is inclined to extend its power at the expense of the monarchy and democracy, then the state in the third millennium should strengthen the two other elements, namely monarchy and democracy. In our democratic age, the monarchy can only be strengthened with democratic legitimation, either by active legitimation, with an elected president in a republic, or by a passive legitimation, through a hereditary monarchy such as in Liechtenstein, where the people can always vote out the monarch and the monarchy.

A hereditary monarchy with democratic legitimation and clearly defined powers in the constitution is less dependent on an oligarchy than a president, who is more or less dependent on the support by the oligarchy for his election and re-election. Furthermore, a hereditary monarchy can pursue a long-term policy, sometimes over generations, rather than the very short-term goals that typify nearly all democracies because of the frequency of elections. Perhaps more important, however, than the question of the type of monarchy are strong direct democracy and the right of self-determination at local community level. Only a strong direct democracy and the end of the state monopoly on its territory will turn the state in the third millennium into a service company that will serve the people. It seems to be the only way to guarantee that the state is not misused by monarchs and oligarchs to oppress and plunder the people. If indirect democracy is the democracy of illiterates, then direct democracy and the right of self-determination at the local level is the democracy of educated people.

10. The state of the future

The modern state is a very complex construction consisting of many systems that have to be in tune with one another. One can compare the state with a large commercial aircraft. The commercial aircraft carries its passengers through space, whereas the state carries its passengers—the people—through time. If the aircraft is badly designed and has a tendency to crash now and then, one tries to rectify the deficiency of the design and does not blame the pilot and the passengers. With states one is inclined to blame the politicians or the people who have chosen them, instead of designing state systems that are as safe as possible and that will give their passengers a better chance of survival if they crash.

What should the state of the future look like, so it can fulfill the needs of humanity in the third millennium in an optimal way? Humanity has been shaped in its genetics and its social behavior by a long history and a long selection process. In order to draft the model for the state of the future, one has to start with the realities of the past, whether we like them or not. Too many state utopias in human history have failed miserably because they began with an idealistic picture of humanity that did not correspond to reality. Communism is just one of those utopias that caused much suffering to people, fulfilling the proverb that the road to hell is paved with good intentions.

Initially through the agrarian and later through the industrial revolutions, states or state-like entities, which were small in size and population, became large states with very large populations. Compared with the long history of humanity, those revolutions took place very quickly, and therefore humanity was unprepared for them both socially and genetically. In the large states monarchs and oligarchs, elected or not, secured a privileged position for themselves and their descendants, first through religious legitimation and later by indirect democratic legitimation, mixed with an ideological legitimation based on nationalism and socialism.

A globalized world shaped by a worldwide communications network and highly efficient transport technology is now experiencing the next step in human history. States are joining together in international organizations to cooperate worldwide in areas of importance for the whole human race. We are living at a time of profound changes, comparable with the transition from hunter-gatherer societies to the agrarian age. The transition to the agrarian age lasted several thousand years. The transition from the agrarian age to the globalized industrial and service society and to the space age is taking place over decades rather than centuries. This is a major challenge for humanity, and one can only hope that it will not end in catastrophe but will be handled successfully.

Two world wars and an enormous increase in knowledge, giving even small groups the possibility of producing weapons of mass destruction, should make us think carefully about our future. As worldwide knowledge of nuclear, bacteriological, and chemical weapons has grown during the last fifty years, so the cost of producing these weapons has fallen. The Nuclear Non-Proliferation Treaty (NPT) has not prevented the rise of new nuclear powers. Even a small state like Israel has, according to reliable intelligence possessed nuclear weapons for years. A very poor state, North Korea, is clearly at the point of becoming a nuclear power. In fifty to a hundred years it may be possible to produce weapons of mass destruction that we cannot even imagine today. In 1930 the leading physicists of their time could not imagine the production of an atomic bomb, but only fifteen years later it was used. Humanity must gradually forget about solving its problems on the battlefield, weapons in hand. There are probably only a few decades left to steer international politics toward avoiding a catastrophe in the third millennium that will make the two world wars seem like minor conflicts.

The challenge for the third millennium will be to develop a state model that fulfills the following conditions:

1. it prevents wars between states as well as civil wars;

2. it serves not only a privileged section of the population but the whole population;

3. it offers the people maximal democracy and the rule of law;

4. it is geared to the competition of the age of globalization.

Those goals can only be achieved if the state is seen as an organization that serves the people and not the other way around. The state has to become a service company facing peaceful competition, and not a monopoly giving the "customer" only the alternatives of accepting bad service at the highest price or emigrating. In this context, one has to remember that in the so-called people's republics of modern history emigration was more or less prohibited, and to flee the republic was a criminal offense punishable by long prison sentences. Many people were killed trying to flee such republics, and in the People's Republic of North Korea this is unfortunately still the case. But even where people are allowed to leave their countries, for the large majority emigration is not an option because the possibilities for immigration have been drastically reduced. In addition, for many people emigration is not an attractive alternative. Before they consider emigration, they are therefore willing to accept many disadvantages, including bad service from the state at an excessive price. The alternative for many desperate and hopeless people is not emigration, but violence, terrorism, revolution, and civil war.

Even in democratic constitutional states, some minorities, rightly or wrongly, feel disadvantaged. One need only think of Northern Ireland, the Basque Country, South Tirol, Québec, or the aboriginal populations of Australia and North and South America. In a democracy, politicians orientate themselves toward the wishes of the majority in order to win elections, which the majority decides. Majority decisions can be unfair and the majority is not always right. A relatively homogeneous majority that defines itself by ethnicity, religion, language, culture, or politics can in particular circumstances bring about "ethnic cleansing" of the state's territory by disadvantaging the minority for so long in the economic, cultural, religious, or political fields that it either emigrates or is assimilated compulsorily. In the United States in the 19th century, a democratic state with the rule of law, the native Indian population was even subjected to massacres in which women and children were not spared.

A state model that is to secure peace, the rule of law, democracy, and the welfare of the population has to give up any claim to a monopoly on its territory. The "emigration" of the population is only a realistic alternative in our world if the affected population can "emigrate" with its territory. For the state to be able to give up its monopoly, the territory has to be divided into small units, so even very small groups of people have the possibility of "emigrating". The smaller the unit, the smaller the probability that the affected population will decide lightly to "emigrate." For very small units it is difficult to create a viable democratic state in which the rule of law is applied and which offers the population better conditions than the old state, when the latter worked reasonably well. Nevertheless, the pressure for political reforms in a state that works badly increases dramatically; otherwise, the state falls apart.

The larger the political units, whether they are called provinces, federal states, or cantons, the greater the danger that they will exercise their right of self-determination and leave the state. There is also a greater danger that inside the new states there will be minorities who are discriminated against and who will one day defend themselves violently. The break-up of Yugoslavia, the Soviet Union, the colonial empires, or the Austro-Hungarian Empire clearly shows the dangers of such developments. However, the smaller the political units that are allowed to exercise their right of self-determination, the smaller is the danger that the state will break apart and that minorities will emerge within it who will be discriminated against.

The smallest political units in most states, which are more or less defined politically and territorially, are local communities such as villages and cities. In the past some local communities such as the city of Berlin were divided, but it is questionable whether that makes much sense. There is much to be said for treating local communities as political units that should not be territorially divided any further. A community can consist of a village with a few hundred inhabitants and a few square kilometers, or a large city with several million inhabitants and several thousand square kilometers. In a local community, disadvantaged minorities can also emerge if the majority of the population votes to withdraw from the existing state. Nevertheless, usually either such minorities are better integrated in their community, or emigration to a neighboring community is easier. In a small community it will always be very difficult to convince a majority of the population that withdrawal from the existing state is the right solution.

For a successful mini-state like the Principality of Liechtenstein with its population of approximately 35,000 and eleven communities, conditions have been extremely favorable both historically and geographically. In the past, even in Liechtenstein, there were some who doubted that sovereignty and the associated right of self-determination made any sense. Nevertheless, there was always a clear majority of the Liechtenstein people who wanted to maintain the country's sovereignty, for example, in the critical years between 1938 and 1945, when the Third Reich was our neighbor. In the last analysis, however, the sovereignty of the Principality of Liechtenstein was only preserved over the centuries because of close and good relationships with the two neighboring states and the political and financial support of the Princely House. Other independent political units in the neighborhood, which still existed in the Middle Ages, were integrated into either Switzerland or Austria.

The right of self-determination, and therefore of sovereignty, at the level of local communities is certainly the most unusual and controversial proposition in the new model for a state in the third millennium. The majority of today's oligarchs who command a privileged position in existing states will fight it tooth and nail. Yet those members of the oligarchy who look beyond the next election might perhaps recognize that they too have some chances in the new state and might even count themselves among the winners. A state that is politically decentralized and more competitive in the age of globalization is in their interest too. Even if an old state breaks apart peacefully because it has lost its competitive edge in the eyes of the population, the old oligarchies have a good starting position if they join the process of independence early enough.

Let's take a glimpse into a distant future, when the states of this world have become service companies that are in peaceful competition for potential customers. There the customer is king and can choose, just as he can choose today whether he wants to buy a hamburger at McDonald's or Burger King or fry it himself, or choose what airline he wants to fly with, or whether he prefers to travel by car or rail. We need to ask the question: What duties are left to the state in the third millennium that cannot be solved better and more cheaply by private enterprise or by communities themselves?

10.1 The constitutional state

With the exception of foreign policy, the only area where the state, in my opinion, still has a competitive advantage compared to private enterprise, local communities, or associations of communities, is the rule of law. For the vast majority of the population, the most important task of the state is to offer them legal protection, or law and order. Most people are willing to pay a high price for this, either financially or by giving up some of their freedom and political rights. When anarchy looms, the call follows for a strong man or dictator, who is then supposed to rule with an iron fist. Whoever wants to have democracy and the rule of law will see that the maintenance of law and order is by far the most important task of a state, long before it has taken over all the other tasks.

To build a constitutional state and to maintain the rule of law is a constant challenge in a globalized world with the high mobility of people, goods, and information. If one looks at the explosive growth of laws and regulations over the last fifty years in the highly developed democracies, one sees that those laws and regulations are slowly filling whole libraries. Nevertheless, the citizen is supposed to know all these laws and regulations, and if he unwittingly breaks one of them he can be punished—ignorance of the law is no defense. Another problem is that these laws and regulations sometimes contradict one another. If a person or a company respects one law, he or it might break another one. Even judges, lawyers, and the state administration have lost their overview, not to mention the legislators. Moreover, laws and regulations are changed quite often and are sometimes written in a technical language, which is difficult for the typical citizen to understand. To make matters worse, even in a number of highly developed democratic constitutional states, there is a dangerous lack of personnel who are qualified in law enforcement, public prosecution, and the courts. This is one of the reasons for the difficulty of fighting white-collar crime across borders efficiently and rapidly. As a result, legal proceedings in such cases can go on for years.

The outcome for most democratic constitutional states is that the increase in legal regulations has decreased the legal protection of the citizen. It has become more difficult for the state to protect its citizens against both smaller and more serious crime. As a result, the democratic constitutional state may become a facade and collapse one day. Indeed, it is a small miracle that the rule of law still works in many states. In most cases, we have to be grateful to a number of idealistic individuals who work with much commitment in law enforcement, public prosecution, and the courts, despite the fact that very often they could earn far more money in the private sector.

What is the use of a democratic constitutional state, which has built up the most sophisticated social system or has the most refined cultural policy, when the main pillar of the constitutional state, the rule of law, is crumbling, and the state is unable to offer its citizens decent legal protection? It is therefore vitally important that the state sheds all those other tasks that can be better performed by local communities or private businesses, either because they are nearer to people and their problems or because, unlike the state, they have to compete on the free market.

Politicians and bureaucrats like to state that the market has failed in this or that area. This alleged market failure serves as a reason to produce a constant stream of new rules and laws, ranging from retirement benefits to environmental protection. Yet if the alleged market failure is investigated a little further, it usually turns out to be a state failure. A market can only emerge when there are property rights: if the state fails to protect such property rights by law or regulations, there is no market. Property rights are very often created by state laws.

Here again, it is worthwhile to look at human history. The hunters and gatherers of the Stone Age, for instance, did not own land that could be bought or sold by the individual but only hunting grounds, used and defended by the whole tribe. The state or the tribe intervened and issued rules for its usage if common property, which was used by everybody, became scarce and valuable. In the agrarian society and the agrarian state, the individual could own land as property to be used and traded. Property rights were issued for land, for mineral rights, and for hunting and fishing rights. In our time, deep-sea fishing is a good example of how rights of usage or property emerged. Everybody was allowed to catch fish in the open sea as long as there were more than enough fish. When fish stocks started to decline over the past few decades, states expanded their territorial waters along the coast and restricted fishing. One of the difficulties of deep-sea fishing is how to regulate the exploitation of fish stocks in such a way that property rights and efficient markets emerge.

If a common good like deep-sea fishing, which has previously been practiced without restriction, is simply restrained by laws and regulations, the freedom of the individual is restricted. Such a system of laws and regulations compels the state continuously to check whether they are being followed. This is expensive and costs taxpayers money. In addition, such a system is prone to corruption and other misuses. A market with property rights that can be traded creates wealth for the individual and is more or less self-regulating. The state has only to supervise the market and, if required, to change only one regulation or other, which costs the taxpayer much less. The allocation of resources through a market is much fairer and more efficient than by a large, slow, and often corrupt state bureaucracy where personal connections can be more important than economic competence. Luckily, in a number of states it appears that a slow change of direction toward a market-regulated system is taking place, even where the environment is concerned.

In order to design the democratic constitutional state for the third millennium, one should start with those authorities that produce the laws and regulations. They include, among others, parliaments, state administrations, governments, and the people where there is direct democracy. In this context I remember the remark of someone who knew the whole process of legislation very well: "The production of laws is like the production of sausages. It is better not to look at the process from nearby, as it is unappetizing, but rather to look at the result." As a head of state I have had occasion to look at this process from nearby on a national and international level and have to add that unfortunately the "sausages" are often unappetizing too.

With the exception of Great Britain and New Zealand, all democratic constitutional states have a written constitution as a basis for their legislation. In this constitution the organization of the state and the fundamental rights of citizens are written down. If the tasks of the state are essentially reduced to the rule of law and foreign policy, a short and easily comprehensible constitution becomes possible. This has the advantage of making it much easier for citizens to know and to use it. Unfortunately, most constitutions that I am familiar with are quite long and difficult to understand. There are even some people responsible for legislation, such as members of parliament, who do not know the constitution of their own state.

The requirement that the legislator should write clearly and concisely should not only apply to the constitution but also to all the laws and regulations with which normal citizens have to comply. If the state expects citizens to know the constitution and the laws, it is the state's duty to inform them about the constitution and the laws that are in force. In this connection, it cannot be stressed enough that the state should be a service company, which has to serve citizens, and not the other way around. Children in school have to learn many subjects, some of which are of doubtful utility. Should it not be the task of the state to ensure that schools should also teach the law? Should not the state give each citizen a compendium of laws, which contains the constitution and the most important laws, together with a commentary, so that citizens can find their way in the constitutional state and know their rights and duties?

Of course, there are a large number of laws and regulations that citizens do not have to know in daily life but that are nevertheless necessary, for instance, to protect the consumer and the environment against harmful products. These regulations are aimed at companies in the industrial, agricultural, and service sectors. The large number of regulations is a burden, especially for small companies. At the same time, those small companies are extremely important for employment and innovation in a national economy. Besides high taxation, complicated tax and social laws, and regulations that change all the time, are important reasons why small companies are not set up in the first place or fail quickly. Since companies pay direct and indirect taxes, duties, social security contributions, etc., to public authorities at the state or community level, it should be the legal duty of these authorities to advise companies on such matters more or less free of charge. If regulations are contradictory, those regulations that favor the taxpayer and the companies should apply. Only then will the state and the local communities serve the people and not rob them. If the state issues tax laws that are unclear or contradictory, it should be liable and not the taxpayer.

It is not only the national production of laws and regulations that has increased dramatically, but also the number of regulations created as a result of bilateral agreements between states, membership in regional organizations such as the European Union, and participation in global organizations such as the United Nations. In theory, the national legislature should also deal with this large legal field and determine which international regulations should be applied on the national level and if so, how. However, anyone who has dealt with this legal area knows that the national legislature is usually not competent to fulfill this task, and that international law is implemented in such a poor manner that it is often in conflict with existing law.

If the constitutional state, whether democratic or not, turns out to be unable to cope with these problems, it might well disappear one day in its present form. I have been able to follow this unpleasant development closely over the decades. As a young man I had the chance to work in the office of an American senator—Senator Claiborne Pell from Rhode Island—in Washington, DC. Despite the fact that being an American senator is a full-time job and that each senator has a staff of qualified people, it was even then hardly possible for a senator to maintain an overview of all the laws, treaties, regulations, and other decisions made by the Senate. What was already the case in the 1960s for a full-time senator and his staff is even more so today for all parliaments, especially for those whose members do not work full-time and who do not have a staff of qualified people. In legislation the constitutional reality has deviated from the written constitution, which puts the credibility of the whole constitutional state at risk.

What would a reform of law-making look like, which could bring this essential process in a constitutional state back to the basic principles of a democratic constitution? It is critical that the state focus on its most important task, to maintain the rule of law, and give up gradually all those other tasks that have been assigned to it over the past two hundred years by nationalistic and socialistic ideologies. The transfer of all those tasks to private business or to local communities would make it possible to reduce the number of laws and regulations and to concentrate, as far as possible, on more general legal guidelines. Local communities are much closer to problems such as social security and welfare, and problems can usually be recognized at an earlier stage and solved faster without countless regulations and a large bureaucracy. Complicated and extensive laws and regulations at state level are often necessary because they have to take into account all kinds of special cases which have no relevance in most communities. If they do become relevant, they can be solved in a fast and unbureaucratic way without establishing precedents for other communities.

A strict self-limiting of the state in the constitution would make it more difficult and, in some cases, impossible for parties and politicians to "buy votes" before each election with all kind of new promises. Apart from the large number of new laws created thereby, such promises also result in high costs. Billions are promised for the conservation of old industries and billions more for the creation of new industries. The collection of those billions from the poor taxpayer and their distribution to a number of privileged people is a bureaucratic process, which already consumes a certain percentage of this sum. Even for the entrepreneur in his own branch of industry, it is difficult to judge if his investment will be successful. Politicians and bureaucrats are not entrepreneurs and cannot judge whether the enterprises which are receiving those billions of taxpayers' money will survive or not. As a result, most of these billions are lost. Since they had first to be earned by successful companies and hard working people, the whole process becomes an exercise of money destruction, which is taken away from the successful part of the national economy. The healthy part of the national economy is thus weakened, less is invested, and more successful companies and people emigrate. In the end only the politicians, the bureaucrats, and the unemployed are left, and the state collapses.

Only one part of the problem is solved if the constitution limits parliament to dealing only with the main tasks of the state, namely foreign policy and maintaining the rule of law. Even in small states one could argue that members of parliament should be employed full-time and given qualified staff to assist them. This costs money, but the cost of parliament is small compared with the costs it creates through bad laws and the total costs of a state. What is important is that members of parliament can select their own staff and that these are not civil servants who cannot be dismissed and are simply allocated to them.

Another sensible measure would be to keep the number of members of parliament as low as possible. The expectation that members of parliament would be a cross-section of the population and would therefore represent the people turned out to be an illusion from the very beginning. The members of parliament represent their parties; and even if they do not always vote according to the party line, they do not represent a cross-section of the population. With a large parliament the duration of the debate increases, but unfortunately not its quality. A large parliament is also a disadvantage because members do not know one another very well and cooperation becomes more difficult. The larger the parliament, the greater the danger that its main task, legislation, will be taken over by the administration, political parties, the state bureaucracy, or some other group.

It is difficult to say what the optimum size of a parliament should be. It probably differs from one case to another. Whenever there is doubt, a smaller number is better. The parliament of Liechtenstein had for a long time only fifteen members and a few deputy members, none of them full-time. Compared to much larger parliaments, the small Liechtenstein parliament did a good job. Because of the increasing foreign policy obligations of parliamentarians and increasing membership in international organizations, the number of deputies in the Liechtenstein parliament was increased from fifteen to twenty-five in 1988, following a referendum with a very narrow result. The members of the Liechtenstein parliament welcomed the higher number of deputies because it made it easier to fulfill foreign policy obligations but it also made their regular legislative work more complicated.

More important than a large and not very representative parliament is the integration of the people into the process of legislation through direct democracy. As explained in Chapter 8, the Liechtenstein model of direct democracy seems to be superior to the Swiss model. Reservations about a strong direct democracy can be dealt with by giving the head of state the power of veto over decisions taken by popular vote. If the Reigning Prince of Liechtenstein has veto power, there is no reason to deny it to the president of a republic. Both need the trust of the people when they use their veto to prevent a wrong decision by the people. There is perhaps one difference. A monarch who got his job by birth is more independent than a monarch looking for re-election.

One may ask whether a state needs a two-chamber system for its parliament if the tasks of the state are reduced constitutionally to maintenance of the rule of law and foreign policy, and local communities have a high degree of autonomy with the right of secession. A parliament with a two-chamber system is more expensive and the decision process is more complicated. In nearly all states with a two-chamber system, one of the chambers reflects a historic development, which very often has lost its meaning. In the second chamber federal states, cantons, or provinces are usually represented by deputies, regardless of the size of their population. A second chamber is not required if local communities have more autonomy than federal states, cantons, and provinces have now. Within the framework of their larger autonomy, communities will always be free to cooperate inside those traditional regions. One can therefore assume that regions that have developed historically, like the Federal State of Bavaria or the Swiss cantons, will continue to exist and cooperate in many areas in which the state will no longer be active.

In a state that sees itself as a service company for the people, some improvements can be made in law enforcement, such as the police, who have to ensure that the laws and regulations of the state are observed. As mentioned before, laws and regulations that are complicated or contradictory can cause problems for the police. It is difficult for them to enforce unpopular laws because people blame the police, not lawmakers, for these laws. This shortcoming is reduced in a direct democracy because a draft for a law, if it is fully understood by the public and is unpopular, can be rejected in a popular vote.

In a number of states, the police not only complain about a lack of financial and personnel resources but also about a lack of support from the politicians. This should not be a problem in states that focus only on foreign policy and the rule of law. Politicians and parties who fail in those two tasks cannot compensate for this with achievements in other areas and will therefore endanger their re-election. For the voter it will be much easier to make a clear decision, as the whole system becomes more transparent.

What is valid for goods, services, and tourists in a globalized world applies also to criminals, who are highly mobile and can cooperate worldwide. To combat international crime efficiently, international cooperation is required in several areas. The states need highly qualified police officers, who speak several languages and are familiar with different cultures. White-collar criminals, in particular, are active internationally through different companies in different states. The police officers combating economic crimes also require a good knowledge of the international economy. This is expensive, but it would be a mistake to cut costs here, because the costs of white-collar crime internationally are far higher than those of combating it.

In this connection a problem should be mentioned, which is one of the main reasons that international crime has been able to finance a rapid expansion over the last forty years—the drug problem. According to the estimates of international organizations, double-digit billion dollar amounts are earned every year through the production, trade, and distribution of illegal drugs. The profits of the international drug cartels are much higher than the sums states can spend combating the problem. The indirect costs are also enormous. There are the health problems caused directly or indirectly by the consumption of drugs. Drug addicts are very often not able to work, and their treatment and living expenses usually have to be paid by the taxpayer, especially if they have been infected by AIDS, jaundice, or other illnesses. Of special significance for the constitutional state and the police are drug-related crimes used to finance the consumption of drugs. The drug problem has probably been responsible for the large increase in crime in most industrial states over recent decades, and an end is not in sight.

States basically have three options for dealing with the drug problem:

1. *To continue the current policy of strict prohibition.* This policy has not only clearly failed, but it has enabled the drug cartels to build a worldwide distribution network, better than Coca-Cola's, with the help of large profit margins, which are many times those of any legal business. The distribution network of the drug cartels reaches into the smallest villages, not despite worldwide policy on drugs, but because of it. After the First World War, a strict prohibition policy against alcohol in the United States failed miserably after a few years. Nevertheless, this failed policy of prohibition continues to be maintained with regard to other drugs.

2. *To legalize and lift all controls on illegal drugs.* It is doubtful whether this is politically feasible or desirable today. A number of scientific studies have indicated that illegal drugs are more damaging for at least the majority of people than alcohol.

3. *To combat illegal drugs by primarily respecting the laws of a market economy and treating drug addicts.* The success of such a strategy depends on whether states are willing to pay the producers, who are mainly poor farmers in developing countries, a higher price than the drug cartels for the raw materials used to produce illegal drugs. Drug addicts would have to be able to obtain drugs at a much lower price than they can buy them from the drug cartels. Since the cartels have to work illegally, their costs for production, transport, and distribution are significantly higher than for a legal and efficient organization. The fight against the illegal drug business has to be carried out until the business loses its profitability for the cartels. Drug addicts should be allowed to consume drugs in locations where they are supervised by qualified personnel, who inform them about the danger of drug consumption and advise them about possible therapies. The total cost of such a program would be much lower than the costs now incurred by the policy of strict prohibition. Perhaps it would even be possible to cover part of the costs, if the sales price for the drug addicts included a profit margin. The consumer of illegal drugs cannot expect that all the costs of his addiction should be met by the taxpayer. Drug-related crimes would more or less disappear with such a strategy, the cities would become safer, and the police could focus on other tasks. Perhaps those politicians, especially from the United States, who rightly preach to the whole world the advantages of a market economy, will finally recognize that the laws of the market economy cannot be simply ignored in the policy toward illegal drugs.

The state will never be able to prevent the abuse of drugs completely. However, it is certainly not the duty of the state and the authorities to encourage this abuse by regulations that ignore the laws of a market economy. The present policy of strict prohibition undermines not only the rule of law in industrial states but also, in a much more dramatic way, the rule of law in less developed countries. The billions of dollars of profit earned every year through the production, trade, and distribution of illegal drugs finance not only organized crime but also terrorist organizations and guerrilla warfare in Third World countries. High ideals and the best intentions have led to the present policy on drugs, but if one looks at the result, one gets the impression that they have been misguided. If there were a Nobel Prize for stupidity, the inventor of this policy on drugs could be considered a good candidate.

A state that transfers many tasks to local communities must also grant them the authority to issue their own regulations based on local requirements and give them the ability to monitor these regulations. Regulations on traffic, the environment, municipal planning, social security, building codes, and many other areas could be made by local communities within a wider legal framework. Perhaps the laws and regulations issued by communities or local associations would be better monitored by officials and police who report to and are paid by the communities or the regional authorities. In some cases it might be advantageous to put a private company in charge of those tasks, as is already the case in some states where private companies act under the supervision of the state authority.

In a state that considers itself a service company for the people, civil servants should behave towards their customers—the people and the local communities—like employees in a well-run service company. In a state whose main task in domestic policy is the rule of law, the policeman will usually be the most important representative of the state for most citizens. In this respect, great progress has been achieved in many democratic states. The slogan "the police, your friend, protector, and helper" has been put into effect to a large extent. Among many other tasks, policemen teach traffic regulations to children in schools and advise house owners on how to protect themselves against burglars. If one compares the service provider state with a business, such as a restaurant, then the policeman is the waiter and the legislature the kitchen. The guests will only be happy and come back if the service is friendly and efficient, the food is good, and the prices low.

A state based on the rule of law not only needs a legislature and law enforcement, but just as important it also needs an independent justice system. The court organization of a future state can rely on the well-tested models of modern constitutional states:

1. the *normal courts* with their usual first, second, and third instances;

2. a *constitutional court*, which has to decide whether the laws, regulations, and decisions of the state or local communities are in accordance with the constitution;

3. an *administrative court*, to which individuals or companies affected by a decision of either the state or a community administration can appeal.

With the introduction of the constitution of 1921, the Principality of Liechtenstein became one of the first constitutional states in the world to put this concept of a comprehensive court system into practice. Liechtenstein was able to follow closely the model developed and introduced by the new Austrian republic. Legal developments in Austria always had and still have a strong influence in the Principality of Liechtenstein. The constitutional reform of 2003 took into account not only the experiences of the previous eighty years in the Principality of Liechtenstein, but also those in Austria and other states. A future state in the third millennium, even if much larger than the Principality of Liechtenstein, should be able to use the same basic concept and organization for its court system.

The challenge in most states is not defining what an efficient court organization should look like, but rather securing the independence of individual judges from party politics and other pressure groups. Direct intervention by politicians in decisions by judges is rare and difficult to prove. Nevertheless, many judicial decisions can only be explained as behaviour to please politicians, which can be characterized as anticipatory obedience. One reason is that political parties and special interest groups can have considerable influence on the appointment of judges.

Anyone who has studied court decisions that are politically sensitive, with state interests at stake, will notice that even in democratic constitutional states, courts make decisions that contradict the wording and the meaning of the law. Those decisions are written so that only the expert will recognize them as clearly contrary to the law. It is then nearly impossible to explain to the general public that the court has intentionally decided against the law to protect certain interests, with state interests often used only as an excuse. Such behavior sooner or later puts the credibility of the constitutional state and the rule of law in question—and not only with the experts.

The main problem is that the oligarchy of political parties occupies all the key positions in a state, from the legislature through the executive branch to the justice system. When, in addition, the state has taken over many tasks compared to earlier centuries and has become the dominant force in the economy, the freedom of the individual citizen is slowly eroded until only a facade is left. The solution in Liechtenstein for the election of judges, as described in Chapter 8, combined with a radical reduction of state duties to foreign policy and maintenance of the rule of law, is one way of averting this danger.

The dismissal of judges, as well as their appointment, is a difficult subject. Even with the most careful selection there will always be judges who are no longer up to their task. A person changes over time. Intellectual or physical strength becomes weaker and some features of character might emerge that may make the person unsuitable for the position of a judge.

Even in democratic constitutional states, people are appointed as judges for political reasons, when it is fairly clear that they are not suited to this role. I have direct experience of such a case in Liechtenstein. The judge was unable to make decisions, and undecided court cases piled up on his desk over the years. People first complained to the politicians but without success, because the judge was politically very close to the majority party at that time. Finally, the people came to me as their head of state. After years of effort, and after the judge had caused more problems for the state in the field of international cooperation in law enforcement, it was finally possible, with all forces combined, to send him into early retirement. In a small state such as Liechtenstein, such problems are usually recognized earlier than in larger states, and if there is the political will these problems can also be solved faster. Nevertheless, even a small state needs controls to recognize such problems at an early stage. In order to remove an incapable judge from office, procedures are required that are transparent and comprehensive but that also protect the privacy of the affected person. Anyone who has to deal with international cooperation in law enforcement knows that even between European democratic constitutional states there are major differences in the efficiency of the legal system.

Another problem in most constitutional states is that there are not enough judges, so that many court cases drag on for years. The shortage of qualified law enforcers, state prosecutors, and court staff leads to a de facto denial of the law by the state for its citizens. Some cases are no longer investigated, even if there is a well-founded suspicion that a serial murderer is at large, as was the case not long ago in Belgium.

The Council of Europe is supposed to defend the principles of the democratic constitutional state in Europe at the highest level, but even there the situation is not satisfactory. The Council of Europe loves to give unsolicited advice about human rights and the principles of the democratic constitutional state both inside and outside Europe. This same Council of Europe has a European Court of Justice concerned with human rights, where over the years around 90,000 charges, often involving serious breaches of human rights, have not been dealt with. As if this were not already cause enough for concern, this same European Court of Justice, which is apparently completely overworked, finds the time to deal extensively with cases that do not fall within its jurisdiction but are important to some influential politicians. I have been able to observe closely in a number of cases that affected the Principality of Liechtenstein how the Council of Europe was breaching its own principles on the democratic constitutional state. The Austrian professor Günther Winkler, one of the leading German-speaking experts on constitutional and European law, has recently published a book in which he carefully investigated one of these cases (*The Council of Europe: Monitoring Procedures and the Constitutional Autonomy of the Member States*, Springer, Vienna and New York, 2005).

Squeezed between a growing European Union, the OSCE (Organization for Security and Cooperation in Europe), and the UN, the Council of Europe has lost much of its significance for its member states. The Council of Europe can, in principle, choose between three alternatives: a fundamental reform to regain its credibility when defending the basic principles of the democratic constitutional state; dissolution, because a Council of Europe which is supposed to defend the basic principles of the democratic constitutional state, but is now breaching its own principles and legal procedures, is doing more harm than good; or maintenance of the status quo. Realistically, however, there will be neither fundamental reform nor a dissolution of the Council of Europe. As in the past, it will continue to serve the member states as an institution that supplies jobs and incomes to politicians, civil servants, and experts, paid by the European taxpayer.

European states, together with the United States, were the worldwide pioneers in the development of the democratic constitutional state in the 19th and 20th centuries. On both sides of the Atlantic, however, we now see signs of an erosion of the constitutional state. If it erodes here, what will happen in other parts of the world where it is still very weak? The politicians and the people from the heartlands of the democratic constitutional state have to realize that they have a worldwide responsibility. They have to free the state from all the unnecessary tasks and burdens with which it has been loaded during the last hundred years, which have distracted it from its two main tasks: maintenance of the rule of law and foreign policy. In the democratic constitutional state, the people should be allowed to decide whether the state is to be restricted to its two main tasks. They should vote against all those politicians and parties who try to "buy" votes with the people's own money. If the people allow themselves to be thus corrupted, they cannot be surprised if politicians and parties are corrupt.

The state in the third millennium needs not only the legislature, the police, the institutions which monitor whether the laws are being followed, and the courts, which have to decide if a law has been broken, but also an institution that is usually called the government or executive branch. If the state's responsibilities are drastically reduced, the government can become much smaller. The head of the government is usually a prime minister or chancellor, who chairs the meetings of the government and sets the guidelines for its work. He or she also has the main responsibility for the relationships of the government with the people, parliament, and the head of state, if there is one. The ministry of foreign affairs is responsible for foreign relations and diplomatic representations. The minister for domestic affairs is responsible for the police and all those institutions that have to supervise compliance with the law and regulations. The minister for justice is responsible for the administration of the judicial system—so the courts can work in an efficient way—as well as for state attorneys and prosecutors. The ministry of justice also has to assist the government and parliament with the drafting and amendment of laws. Finally, the minister of finance has responsibility for state finances and tax administration.

In a democracy there are different models for forming and dismissing a government. There are models where the parliament has no influence on the formation of the government. This is the case where the members of the government are elected directly by the people, such as in a number of Swiss cantons, or where the head of government is elected by the people and then has the authority to form his or her own government, as in the United States, where the president is the head of the executive branch and the head of state. Nevertheless, in the United States the members of the government nominated by the president have to be confirmed by the Senate. In other states, either the government is proposed by the head of state to parliament and then elected by parliament, or parliament elects the members of the government who are then appointed by the head of state, if there is one. The head of state has the right in most cases to dismiss the government, to dissolve parliament, and to order new elections.

The different models have their advantages and disadvantages. It is usually difficult for a government without a majority in parliament to realize its program. In the United States and in many Swiss cantons, however, governments without a majority are still able to act and are not too much hindered in their work by an opposing majority in parliament. This is probably because in both these states the parties are not as strong as in other states, and members of parliament therefore have more freedom in their personal decisions. In addition, Switzerland and a number of American federal states have direct democracy, so a blockade in parliament can be bypassed with a popular vote.

More important than the model of government is the question of whether a long-term component, independent of party politics, should be introduced into the political system of a state, in the form of a strong hereditary monarchy like that of the Principality of Liechtenstein. A hereditary monarch is under no obligation to the different parties, and he does not have to take elections into account. Instead, he can concentrate on the long-term welfare of the state and its population. In the Principality of Liechtenstein it has been possible to pursue long-term policies over generations to the benefit of the state and its people. A positive and close cooperation between the different generations of the ruling family has been essential for this.

A question that frequently arises is whether a civil servant can be dismissed like an employee in the private sector. It is important for judges and state attorneys to be independent of politics and political parties, because the latter usually control the legislation through parliament and the executive branch through the government. A state attorney or a judge has to start an investigation and pass a judgment, even if the politicians or public opinion do not agree. The dismissal of a judge or a state attorney should therefore be possible only in exceptional cases and according to regulated procedures.

In a number of states there is a tradition that, like judges, civil servants enjoy de facto lifetime tenure and cannot be dismissed. For states which have no or weak administrative courts, a good case can be made that civil servants, like judges, should be independent. Where comprehensive and independent administrative courts do exist, however, the citizen can bring his case to court, if, in his opinion, the administration has acted arbitrarily or against the law. In such a situation, there is no reason to give civil servants the same rights as judges.

If civil servants had the same independence in their decision-making as judges, they would obtain the discretionary powers that lie in the hands of the government in a democratic constitutional state. A good argument can therefore be put forward that civil servants should be treated like employees in the private sector and that they should not have special protection against dismissal. Of course, if the state is reduced to its main tasks, a massive reorganization of the whole state administration will also be needed. Many civil servants will have the opportunity of moving to the administration of local communities or a region, or transferring into the private sector, should it take over some former state duties. Unfortunately, there will be cases where the employment of a civil servant has to be terminated and he or she has to look for a new position. In the United States, it has always been common practice that a new government replaces most of the top civil servants of the previous administration. A new government needs collaborators whom it can trust and work with so that it can implement at least part of its program, as long as it is carried out within the framework of the constitution and the law. Even in the United States, with its tradition of job rotation between the private and the public sectors, only a small percentage of civil servants are replaced when the government changes.

10.2 The welfare state

As discussed in Chapter 3, social behavior is a fundamental part of human nature. However, should the state of the future maintain the welfare state as it exists today, or perhaps even expand it further?

Our genetically influenced social behavior still corresponds to a large degree to the political and economic structures of hunter-gatherer societies. There, mutual support and the sharing of resources are necessary for the survival of the individual and the group. This system is quite efficient, because social control of the individual by the group is much easier than in a large state. In hunter-gatherer societies the source of wealth is the common territory, which sometimes has to be defended against other groups. Hunter-gatherers harvest, but they do not sow. Personal property is essentially restricted to clothing, weapons, a few household items, and a tent or simple hut.

In the agrarian age, personal ownership of land and with it the means of production had already attained central importance. The farmer now had to till, sow, and harvest his land year in and year out. Nature was still important, but it was no longer the primary producer of wealth. In exchange for the payment of taxes and duties, monarchs and oligarchs, or the state, took on tasks previously handled by the small group or tribe, such as protection against acts of aggression from outside the territory and the maintenance of law and order inside it. Sharing and support remained with the traditional groups such as the extended family, village communities, or the region.

The genetically influenced social behavior of humanity and state structures slowly started to diverge. In villages and small towns, social control, sharing, and support by the group were still possible because everyone knew everyone else. In large cities and states, however, this was no longer possible. Industrialization, migration from the countryside to the cities, and the loss of the extended family and the traditional social structures of the villages accelerated this divergent evolution between genetically influenced social behavior and social structures. In industrialized states, a growing proportion of the population was no longer integrated within traditional social groups. Consequently, the practice of sharing and support was lost, along with the social control exerted by small, traditional social groups. A state with a large population can no longer exert the same kind of control. Attempts to do so lead inevitably to the police state, corruption, and the loss of freedom.

The attempt by communism to return to the hunter-gatherer model of shared and equal distribution of property turned out to be an economic and political catastrophe. The individual was no longer motivated to produce new wealth every year because the state's oligarchy distributed it to others. There was no longer competition over the best methods of producing wealth, but only over how to distribute it. The social behavior of the Stone Age cannot be applied to the social, economic, and political environment of the agrarian and industrialized state.

The social market economy, on the other hand, tries to apply the social behavior of villages and small cities of the agrarian age to the industrialized state by maintaining private property and a market economy. This model has been more successful than communism, but it is also now in crisis and will eventually fail. The welfare state tries by legal means to apply the social behavior of the traditional small group to the whole population. A large bureaucracy is required to manage and control this process. Apart from its high cost, the system threatens the freedom of the individual and in a democracy gives political parties the possibility of "buying" votes with taxpayers' money. The welfare state faces a crisis in the age of globalization with the rapidly increasing mobility of people, services, and goods.

In addition, the welfare state faces a moral problem in our worldwide information society. The human being is a social being, who should have compassion for his neighbors, as demanded by Christianity and other religions. However, Christ pointed out to his Jewish fellow citizens that the neighbor could be a stranger and that one should love even one's enemies. Today, should a father of a family in Munich, who works hard and earns well, really consider the civil servant in Berlin as his neighbor? Is it his duty to pay part of his pension so that this neighbor can retire at sixty and enjoy twenty-five years of leisure, be it in Berlin or Florida during the winter? Is this father in Munich not perhaps more a neighbor to some father in a Third World country, whose family is undernourished, deprived of medical care, and threatened by illnesses and injuries that are easy to cure? Is the welfare state perhaps the product of an ideology that favors the few, instead of the principle of "loving thy neighbor"? Are the people not duped into believing that the welfare state and compulsory solidarity will create heaven on earth for the chosen people, whereas the real beneficiaries are just a small, specially selected minority?

As globalization brings the extended family of humanity still closer together, is it socially defensible for states to force their people to subsidize a life of leisure for a small, privileged class? Would it not be more responsible to give individuals and local communities the opportunity of helping the poorest of the poor by individual donations or by supporting well-run communities in the developing world? The amount of money paid in monthly pensions for a single civil servant in Berlin could not only save the lives of dozens of children in Third World countries but could pay for their education as well. Has not state foreign aid in most cases been a waste of taxpayers' money, hurting more than it has helped?

The welfare state has also helped the state oligarchy to have access to the private lives of citizens, to demand higher taxes from them in order to finance the state bureaucracy, and to create mountains of debt, which will burden future generations. Experts have warned for some time that the welfare state in its current form cannot be afforded much longer, but before elections politicians buy votes by promising to expand it further. Until now, the politicians who make these promises could count on generous retirement packages. Pity those politicians who win an election just when deep cuts in welfare are unavoidable.

The problem started at the end of the 19th century, when Chancellor Bismarck promised citizens of the newly formed German Empire a state pension from the age of sixty-five. Sixty-five was, in fact, the life expectancy at that time, and because the pension itself was modest, funding the plan with taxes seemed to be no problem. Since then, however, life expectancy has sharply increased, as have pension payments, while the retirement age has been reduced in many states. In the meantime, almost all industrialized countries have adopted the German system and now share the same financial problems.

Only a few states have been able to ensure that at least a portion of the pension funds are saved ahead of time. But even in these cases, mistakes have been made because of failures either of supervision or of regulation. What has happened in industrialized countries over the last century shows that the management of pensions should not be one of the state's duties. The danger of abuse at the cost of future generations is simply too great.

In addition, state pensions funded by the so-called pay-as-you-go policy are probably contributing to the falling birth rates of most industrial states. In the past, for most people, their children supported them in their old age. Children are not only a source of joy for their parents, but they can also be a burden financially and time consuming. Why should people take on the cost and trouble of having children, when they are required by the state to pay for the pensions of people they do not know, and the state guarantees their own pension? However, an awareness is slowly emerging that the state cannot take on this responsibility because the materialistic fun society, as mentioned before, produces few if any heirs.

For our western civilization, lifelong work means a fundamental shift in attitude, even though the state pension system is a relatively new development. A sudden cessation of state pensions is therefore politically impossible except in a serious crisis. People who are already retired or about to retire need their state pensions to survive, because it would be very difficult for them to find work. However, in those circumstances increases in pension payments above the inflation rate are unjustifiable, because future generations will have to finance their pensions themselves to enjoy the life currently enjoyed by the retired.

In order to prevent greater crises, the retirement age will have to be increased, and the pension system will have to be changed gradually from the current unfunded pay-as-you-go system to a funded system. Once this change has been effected, each individual can decide when to retire. Regulations that make the employment of older workers unattractive must be rescinded. Society will have to come to terms with the fact that increased life expectancy will allow people to work longer. In fact, working past the usual retirement age seems to contribute positively to mental and physical health for as long as the work itself is not too physically taxing. This is an advantage for the individual and his environment. The funded pension system even allows individuals the option of passing on their savings to their children if they partially or even completely forego their pensions.

Opponents of a funded pension system often claim that it is socially undesirable because it only benefits people who can afford to contribute part of their earnings. This is not correct, because a general contribution duty can be required by law, just as in a pay-as-you-go system, which can lead to a redistribution in favor of people with low or no income. In the pay-as-you-go system today, people with a high income already have to contribute more to the costs of the system than those on a low income. People with no income make no contribution and still receive a pension. The question whether the system is funded or unfunded can be completely separated from the question of who finances it.

Opponents of a funded system also argue that private pension systems, especially those run by companies who invest their funds in their own company, are particularly exposed to abuse and loss of capital. In principle, private pension systems run by a company should not be allowed to invest the pension funds in their own company. Unfortunately, however, mismanagement and losses also occur in a state-run pension system. Appropriate regulations and efficient oversight can greatly reduce such problems.

Just as in the private pension system, it would also be possible to institute a minimal insurance covering accidents and sickness with a social component. It would make sense to have a sliding scale of premiums, according to risk factors. Most insurance plans today have surcharges for sports where the risk of injury is relatively high. Similarly, it is unjustifiable to charge everyone the higher costs of insuring those who choose unhealthy lifestyles, such as excessive smoking, eating, drinking, or too little exercise. On the other hand, insuring those with uncontrollable risk factors such as age, gender, or congenital health conditions ought to be a shared responsibility.

Accident and health insurance is always beset by the possibility of excessive expenses and abuse. Patients and doctors share an interest in optimizing medical treatment because both the patient's health and the doctor's income are at stake. Doctors also need to protect themselves from malpractice suits, which can arise from improper diagnosis and treatment. Consequently, patients and doctors are inclined to the medical equivalent of a Rolls Royce. This should not be surprising because a third party, namely the insurance company, carries the costs. Under those circumstances, it is astounding that health care costs are not much higher in industrialized states.

It is, however, possible to reduce excessive expenses and abuses in accident and health insurance. For instance, patients could have an excess, just like other forms of insurance such as automobile insurance. For people whose income is at subsistence level, the public authorities will have to pay for the minimum insurance and the excess. One can ask a car owner to pay the minimum insurance and excess because he can give up his car if necessary. However, it would certainly be against the social, ethical, and religious principles of the state in the third millennium if the poor were required to give up their health.

In many industrial states with generous welfare systems unemployment was for a long time not a major problem. Today, it has become a problem, and will remain so for the foreseeable future because of rapid structural changes in the world economy. The structural changes that resulted in the transition from the agrarian society to the industrial society and from the industrial society to the service society affected not only the individual but sometimes whole sectors of the economy or whole regions. Private unemployment insurance therefore presents a fundamental problem compared with private accident or health insurance. What private insurance company is willing or able to insure farmers in Third World countries against unemployment?

The best insurance against unemployment remains a state economic policy that makes it attractive for companies capable of competing in the globalized economy to create new jobs. In the past, this was only possible with a liberal economic policy with low taxation, little bureaucracy, maintenance of the rule of law, and a well-educated population. It does not seem that this will change very much in the third millennium.

Can the state of the third millennium delegate the support of the unemployed to local communities? In principle the answer is yes, if one looks at the Principality of Liechtenstein with its 35,000 inhabitants. One has to bear in mind, however, that Liechtenstein has applied the liberal economic policy as described above for decades and enjoys today a strongly diversified economy with a substantial number of companies that can compete on world markets without subsidies. Nevertheless, much can be said in favor of transferring responsibility for the unemployed to local communities, even in states whose economy has not yet reached the level of Liechtenstein's. However, before such a transfer of responsibilities to local communities can take place, the state will have to reform the labor market and the unemployment support system.

In many states minimum wages and social security contributions are too high, which makes the creation of new jobs difficult. An important reform goal would be to reintegrate the unemployed into the workforce as rapidly as possible, because experience has shown that the longer someone is jobless, the harder it is to find work.

The high costs of the welfare state are becoming more of a problem as time goes by. On the one hand, young and capable people try to avoid the increasing tax burden by emigrating either physically or financially. On the other hand, the generous welfare state attracts people who are hardly able or willing to finance it but who want to claim its benefits. The obvious discrepancy between the high financial benefits of the welfare state and the comparably ridiculously small amounts needed to save lives in the Third World leads not only to illegal immigration but, over time, causes political tensions, which raise the danger of conflicts throughout the world.

There is much to be said in favor of the state of the third millennium gradually retreating from the welfare system altogether. The first step would be a gradual transition from an unfunded to a funded pension system and a higher retirement age. The second step would be a reform of the labor market. The third step would be to transfer the entire welfare system to the level of the local community.

At local level, the feeling of solidarity is stronger; problems are recognized early and so are solutions. Decisions can be made swiftly and implemented rapidly, and abuses are more easily detected and confronted. It is up to communities to decide how far they want to merge for such tasks into regional associations and how much they want to subsidize their welfare system. If the state transfers the entire welfare system to local communities and the private sector, it will have to create some sort of legal framework and monitor it in order to prevent abuses. Within this framework, local communities should, however, be able to compete and introduce innovative solutions. The Principality of Liechtenstein, with its 35,000 people, is not much larger than a small town and has an efficient welfare system, with the largest part of its pensions financed through a funded pension system. Transferring the welfare system from state to local level will of course require a complete reorganization of the taxation and financial system, which I address in Chapter 10.5.

The globalization of the world economy will lead in the long run to a harmonization of prices for goods and services. The main beneficiary of this worldwide competition is usually the consumer, which from a social point of view is an advantage. In nearly all areas it has so far brought lower prices, higher quality, and more choice. The automobile industry is a good example, in which, at least to a considerable extent, world market prices prevail. Since the opening of markets in Eastern Europe and India, the prices for automobiles have dropped, while quality and choice have increased. Similar examples can be mentioned in the service sector, such as telecommunications or the financial services industry.

World market prices for goods and services mean that over a long period of time, costs have to be adapted so that local enterprises and thus local jobs can be preserved. World market prices for goods and services, therefore, have to lead to world market prices for costs, including labor costs. That the employers and employees affected by this development try to stop it through protectionism can be understood from a human point of view, but such a policy only postpones the social problem and increases it.

The Indian economist Jagdish Bhagwati has often been mentioned as a possible candidate for the Nobel prize in economics. He has studied the effects of globalization on poverty in India and China and reached the conclusion that economic globalization has been an important element in reducing poverty there. He divides his critics into realists and idealists. The realists are those who obtain economic advantages for themselves through protectionism, at the expense of the consumer. As already mentioned, realists can include employers and employees. The idealists, mainly in industrial states, see economic globalization as the cause of nearly all problems in the Third World, from poverty to environmental damage. Realists and idealists have formed a worldwide coalition against economic globalization, whereby idealists can be seen as useful instruments of the realists, who enrich themselves at the expense of the common good. The movement against economic globalization is thus profoundly inequitable: it increases poverty in the Third World without protecting jobs in industrial states in the long term.

Jobs were certainly lost in industrial states during the last few decades through globalization, but many more jobs were lost over the same period through automation in all three traditional sectors of the economy: in the primary sector, agriculture and forestry; in the secondary sector, manufacturing, construction, and mining; and in the tertiary sector, trade, transportation, and service industries. The social problems attributable to globalization and automation cannot be solved through protectionism and the destruction of machinery and computers. On the contrary, such a policy would lead back to an "economic Stone Age," where a state without imports and exports, cut off from a globalized world economy, would be transformed into a "protectionist reservation." Unemployment might be eliminated for a short time because there would be no machinery, no computers, and no automobiles, but the first crop failure would lead to famine. In addition, the productivity of agriculture would decline significantly in the "protectionist reservation" of the enemies of globalization, because modern agriculture is just as dependent on imports as industry.

The best insurance against unemployment is the creation of new jobs in companies that can compete in a globalized world economy. There the education system has to play a central role, as explained in the following chapter.

10.3 The education system

At the beginning of the 19th century, long before the introduction of the welfare state, a number of European states including the Principality of Liechtenstein introduced compulsory school attendance for all children by law. The state and the local communities first built primary schools, then secondary schools, and finally universities. During the 19th and 20th centuries, the public authorities gradually took over the entire education system. Insofar as there were church and private schools, which still existed and were not nationalized, they were mainly integrated into the state school system. If one takes into account that neither a modern economy nor a modern state can be run by illiterate people, state authorities have to concern themselves with the education of their population. In our modern world an illiterate person is very much handicapped. For such a person it is nearly impossible to find a well-paid job.

Nevertheless, it could be questioned whether it should be one of the responsibilities of the future state to run the education system. As with the welfare system, there are good reasons either to privatize the whole system or to delegate it to local communities. The state would still have a duty to establish and monitor the legal framework for the education system. However, management and ownership of the system from kindergarten to university would be the task of private business, local communities, associations of local communities, or a joint venture between private business and individual local communities. As far as the education system is financed by the state, this should be done through a voucher system with the children or their parents as beneficiaries. Politically, it would not be a very popular system, but it would give children equal opportunities whether they are from poor or rich families.

The philosophy behind an education system financed through vouchers is that today public authorities, be they the central or local government, finance the education system through direct subsidies from kindergarten to university.

This is an inefficient and very often unfair system. Families who have the bad luck to live in an area where the schools are poor have to accept the fact that their children will receive a bad education unless the family can pay for an expensive private school. This is very inequitable, but fits into a nationalistic and socialistic ideology that supports all kinds of state institutions with taxpayers' money but prevents or hinders private institutions.

Instead of using taxpayers' money to finance the education system, it is much better to subsidize parents or students so that they can themselves choose the school that in their opinion is best for them. Well-managed schools which are able to meet the expectations of the parents and the students will be successful. The others will have to adapt or they will disappear from the market. In order to prevent abuse by parents and schools, the subsidies should not be paid in cash, but rather in vouchers, which are redeemed in those schools that fulfill a minimum standard. Parents should only be allowed to cash in vouchers if they make a commitment to the state that they will educate their children themselves or privately. A number of states already release children from compulsory school attendance, if it can be proven that the children will receive an education equal to that provided in a publicly maintained school.

Schools, like other institutions managed and owned by the public authorities, tend to become bureaucratic and inefficient sooner or later. Politicians are reluctant to dismiss headmasters or teachers who no longer fulfill their responsibilities. In many cases, dismissal is very difficult and in a number of states is only possible after long public court proceedings. Politically influential teachers' unions are a further obstacle to an efficient school system. In their minds the welfare of the teacher is, of course, more important than the welfare and progress of the pupils. The political resistance to voucher systems is usually organized and supported by these powerful unions.

The fact that an increasing number of parents and students are willing to pay substantial amounts of money for education in private schools and universities shows that in many cases the public education system does not always meet their expectations. Nevertheless, despite their financial sacrifices, the state forces them to pay taxes to support an inefficient school system that they do not want to use. Even after the introduction of a general voucher system, it will take some time for all parents and students to be completely free to choose schools and universities, because a number of years will be required to establish a comprehensive education system on a purely private basis.

The state of the future should, and will, continue to play an important role in a voucher system, but this is a role that will support social justice in society and not hinder it, in contrast to the education system today. The legal framework set by the state through law or decree will have to clarify a number of questions such as the minimum value of a voucher, how long parents are legally entitled to it, and what the minimum standards for schools should be.

Local communities should have the freedom to decide for themselves if they want to use their tax revenues for a more generous education system and increase the value of the vouchers or use them for their welfare system, culture, or in some other areas. Some local communities might prefer to have lower taxation because they want to maintain or create jobs. Those are all decisions that directly influence the lives of citizens and therefore should be kept as close to the citizen as possible. They should be dealt with via direct democracy at community level and not by a remote authority with restricted indirect democracy.

The people of the Principality of Liechtenstein, with its small population, have been making those decisions for a long time at state and local levels, either directly by popular vote or indirectly through their representatives in the state parliament and the local parliaments of the eleven communities. Are the people of Liechtenstein so much more intelligent than the people of other states? As much as I take pride in the Liechtenstein people, I am convinced that other people are just as intelligent as we are. Those politicians who have doubts and believe that their people are incapable of direct democracy and local autonomy are cordially invited to commission a scientific study to see if their people are less intelligent than the people of Liechtenstein. However, even if this were the case, there is no reason for a democratic constitutional state to deny its people the right to decide how their own tax money should be used in areas that affect them and their families directly.

10.4 Transportation

Should transportation be a duty of the state? Nationalists of the last century with few exceptions took it for granted that the state needed national highways, national waterways, national railroads, national airlines, a national automobile industry, a national airplane industry, and so on. This policy of national transportation has wasted hundreds of billions of taxpayers' money worldwide and still continues to waste them today. Very small states like the Principality of Liechtenstein have fortunately never been able to afford such wasteful, expensive infrastructures at the cost of the taxpayer, with the exception of road construction.

It would be an interesting intellectual experiment to imagine what the world would look like today, if the state, in Europe and elsewhere in the world, had not interfered so aggressively with transportation over the last two centuries. A fundamental change came about almost 200 years ago with the development of the railroad. The 19th century saw the creation of a number of private railroad companies that built financially successful rail networks. Politicians recognized their importance and became involved—naturally with the best interests of the nation in mind. Governments either took complete control of railroad companies, or they were so overregulated that they could no longer compete with the automobile industry which was emerging at the beginning of the 20th century. In addition, the railroad companies had to finance the building and maintenance of the rail network themselves, whereas the road networks were constructed and maintained with taxpayers' money. This is just one of the many examples where politicians distort competition with regulations and taxpayers' money without thinking of the long-term consequences.

Had the state not interfered, the railroad companies with their rail networks would have progressed much more rapidly, rather than stagnating technically for nearly a hundred years at a time when cars and airplanes experienced rapid development. Without intervention, transportation would probably have relied much more on railways, which would be more favorable for the people and the environment than the present system. As a result, the world has been covered by a dense network of roads, over which an avalanche of cars rolls, which not only leaves people dead or injured in its path but also pollutes the environment with exhaust fumes and noise.

Transportation is one of the factors influencing where people live. A system of transportation that relies on well-developed railroads rather than on a road system would encourage a different pattern of settlement, one which would consist of large and small cities linked by high-speed trains. Electric cars would not have been replaced by cars powered by gas or diesel but would have been able to satisfy requirements within the cities, where trips are only short distances at low speeds. A railroad network for high-speed trains requires less land than roads and also handles a larger volume of traffic at much higher speeds. Railways can run on electricity without exhaust fumes, and noise can be controlled far more easily and cheaply than with highways. High-speed trains can replace air travel for medium-range distances, further reducing air and noise pollution near today's airports, which are a problem for both people and the environment.

The dense network of roads financed by taxpayers has contributed to preserving the pattern of settlement of small villages from the agrarian age to our time. This pattern causes very high infrastructure costs such as transportation, education and health care systems, electricity, water, and telecommunications. People in the countryside have limited employment options, leading to strong political pressure to maintain jobs in agriculture with high costs for the taxpayer and the consumer. According to various surveys, it is estimated that in the OECD (Organization for Economic Cooperation and Development) states, this agricultural policy costs taxpayers and consumers approximately one billion dollars per day.

Apart from these costs, state intervention in agriculture has additional disadvantages for consumers and taxpayers. High prices and subsidies permit over-cultivation, particularly in regions not suited to farming, which is a serious burden on the environment. Rivers have been straightened, wetlands drained, and prairies turned into farmland in order to increase agricultural production. The consequence is agricultural overproduction, which the state has either to dump at subsidized prices on the world market or to destroy, with the taxpayer footing the bill.

Only now is a shift in thinking beginning. Environmentalists are criticizing intensive over-cultivation, especially in Europe. Third World countries are becoming aware that cheap agricultural products from industrialized countries, which are sometimes even given away for free, are destroying indigenous agriculture. Farmers in the Third World cannot compete with the subsidized agriculture of the developed world, either on the world market or in the domestic market, which increases their poverty even more. The damage to the Third World caused by this agricultural policy is difficult to estimate. It could be as large as the above-mentioned costs for consumers and taxpayers in the OECD states.

The most reasonable solution, without a doubt, would be free trade worldwide in agricultural products, as there is already in most industrial products. This would benefit taxpayers, consumers, and the environment in the industrial states, as well as farmers in developing countries and the world economy as a whole. Farmers in industrialized states would initially be at a disadvantage. But in the industrialized world, the large decline in the farming population is well behind us, and despite huge subsidies, only a small percentage of the population still lives off agriculture. This percentage will fall further over the next few years, with or without subsidies, because the farming population is quite old, and for many farms there are no successors willing to take over the family business.

The real opening up of markets in OECD states for agricultural products from the Third World and the worldwide introduction of a market economy for agricultural products would encounter considerable political resistance. Some transitional aid would be necessary for those farmers in OECD states who cannot survive on the world market. Some might argue that it is unfair to favor farming over other professions that have become obsolete over the last hundred years. Shoemakers, tailors, blacksmiths, or coachmakers have, with few exceptions, lost their professions, without costing consumers and taxpayers many billions of dollars per annum. Nevertheless, it is much cheaper to retrain or retire farmers early than to keep the current system, which causes such enormous costs worldwide.

Unfortunately, politics are frequently based more on emotions than intelligence. In spirit humanity still appears to live in the agrarian age and it is only today that small changes are noticeable. The loss of landscape molded by the agrarian age can be a problem even for city people, who know the farm with its fields, meadows, and cows only from picture books and television. For communities who wish to keep their agrarian landscapes for tourism or any other reason, it will be much cheaper to employ farmers as landscape gardeners. Then one will still be able to visit the farmhouse from picture books and sentimental movies. Other agricultural land can be converted into parkland for recreation.

Agricultural land in the industrial states that can compete globally will continue to be farmed. Intensive agriculture will develop further to supply consumers with all the products they want. If consumers want products grown without artificial fertilizers or other chemicals, modern agriculture will supply them. Without state intervention, agriculture can and will survive in industrial nations, but only as long as it can provide customers with the products they desire.

This discussion of agricultural policy in the OECD nations may give the impression that today's failed policy is the consequence of yesterday's unwise transportation policy, which favored the automobile over the railroads. However, the opposite is probably true: our thinking, shaped by the agrarian age, produced a transportation policy that was aimed at an agrarian society and not at the industrial and service society of today. Apart from that, roads have been important since ancient times from a military point of view. The state in the third millennium will have to solve the problem not only of how to stop a senseless agricultural policy that costs the consumer and taxpayer billions, but also of how it can retreat from a transportation policy that also costs billions, burdens the environment with noise and polluted air, requires large land areas, and encourages urban sprawl.

Fortunately, modern technology may offer solutions. Electronically charged tolls can be used not only on highways but also on normal roads. The whole road system could be privatized and the burden of direct and indirect costs could be placed directly on drivers, who incur the costs in the first place. A surcharge could be applied to roads where noise pollution is particularly problematic and with which the property owners most affected could be compensated. A privatized railway system could again compete with a privatized road system, which has to bear all its direct and indirect costs. Gradually, systems of transportation and settlement patterns could develop in the direction they would have taken without the massive interference of the state over the past hundred to two hundred years.

Small cities, which a person can easily cross by foot and which lie in a park landscape, would offer a high quality of life. Infrastructure costs would be lower than in today's mega-cities and agrarian settlement patterns that cover large land areas with a low population density. If those small cities were linked by high-speed trains, a network of small cities could be created, which together could offer their inhabitants a wide range of jobs, education, and cultural and sporting opportunities, comparable to a large city but at lower costs and with a higher quality of life.

10.5 Public finances

The question of how the state of the future will finance itself is of critical importance. State finances have to be fundamentally reconsidered if the obligations of the state are limited primarily to maintaining law and order, conducting foreign policy, and financing education. The state will have to transfer the major part of its tax revenues and its tax sovereignty to local communities, if these are to take over additional tasks. There is much to be said for leaving indirect taxation, such as a value added or sales tax, to the state, and giving local communities authority over all direct taxation, such as real estate, corporate, or individual taxes.

A constitutional state with its own foreign policy is a separate economic area, even if it is fully integrated into the world economy through membership of the World Trade Organization (WTO) and into the European economy through membership of the EU. As far as customs duties are concerned, they have to be collected by the state or an organization like the EU, which has received its authority from the member states. It would not make much sense to give this kind of authority to the individual local community. Indirect taxes on goods and services, such as a value added or sales tax, are also more effectively collected by the state, because otherwise there would be distortions in competition that would damage the whole economy. In such a case, goods and services would be manufactured and sold not in the best location for production or where the customer is, but where the taxes are the lowest.

In the United States, control of indirect taxation, the so-called "sales tax," lies with the governments of the federal states and local authorities. This makes taxation on many products and services more difficult. For example, although there was no sales tax in Texas during the 1970s, the sale of alcohol in the eastern part of the state was heavily taxed and restricted. Eastern Texas has a border with Arkansas, which had a high sales tax but no special tax on alcohol. Many years ago, I made a business trip to the city of Texarkana, which straddles the border between Texas and Arkansas. The main street of Texarkana is the border between the two states, and it was easy to see the consequences of the tax policy. All the car dealers had their showrooms on the Texas side of the street, whereas on the other side, in Arkansas, were all the restaurants, bars, and shops that sold alcohol. Customers from far outside the city of Texarkana would travel quite a distance to buy their cars or to drink there. The market distortions were obvious.

Compared to direct taxation it is much easier to raise indirect taxes within a jurisdiction. Much can be automated and the state needs only a relatively small bureaucracy for this task. A centralized administration for indirect taxation is the most practical solution, even if the tax authority remains with the local communities. For this reason the authority to raise indirect taxes should remain with the state and the authority to raise direct taxes with local communities.

There have been a number of publications about the rate of indirect taxation such as value added tax. A uniform tax rate seems to be more important than the actual level of the rate. Nevertheless, politicians love to apply different tax rates, with the surprising justification that this is socially fairer. The highest tax rate is applied to luxury goods, as defined by politicians, while lower tax rates are applied to other goods and services, some of which are even exempt from indirect taxation. This turns the rather simple system of indirect taxation into a complicated one that needs additional civil servants. This, of course, gives politicians the opportunity to employ their friends and fellow party members. It also gives politicians and parties unlimited possibilities to "buy" votes, not by handing out taxpayers' money but through tax advantages. The influence of the state on the economy and with it the influence of politicians is increased, because the politician can now put this product or that service into this or that tax bracket.

Different rates of indirect taxation have as little to do with social justice as the devil has to do with holy water. The wealthy benefit more from lower taxation rates on certain products and services because they consume more than the poor. Poor people from time to time also consume products or services that politicians have defined for reasons best known to themselves as luxury goods. Social policy conducted via variable indirect tax rates costs both the state and the taxpayer a significant amount of money. Direct help for poor people is much more effective.

If the authority for direct taxation lies with local communities and for indirect taxation with the state, there are good social, political, and economic reasons not only for a uniform tax rate but also for a rather high tax rate. Indirect taxation will then be the only instrument for a limited redistribution of income between richer and poorer regions of a state.

A state whose responsibility is restricted primarily to foreign policy and maintenance of the rule of law needs less tax revenue. With high revenues from indirect taxation, the state should achieve a substantial surplus. Part of the surplus will be needed to service the national debt and to repay it over a period of time. The state should also sell all state property which is no longer needed for its main tasks, in order to pay back the national debt as quickly as possible. Income from the sale of national property could also flow into retirement funds to change the pension system as soon as possible into a funded pension system as described in Chapter 10.2. This would facilitate the transformation of the pension system. Nevertheless, the main objective should be to free the state of debts, so that the surplus from indirect taxation can be distributed fully to local communities according to the number of their inhabitants. These per capita allocations of surplus revenue from indirect taxation should give local communities the possibility of covering at least part of their expenses. The rest has to be covered by direct taxation or other income.

Such a division of tax authority would have another major advantage: local communities and the whole population within the state would have a strong vested interest in the state behaving as economically as possible and not increasing its debt. Only then would local communities and their populations benefit from the surpluses of indirect taxation. The population has much better control over the use of taxpayers' money at local community level, particularly where there is direct democracy, than it does at national level.

Such a division of tax authority could stop the trend toward the continuous strengthening of the central power to the detriment of local communities and regions, which can be seen again and again in human history. As soon as the state tries to extend its political influence by taking over additional tasks, it reduces the income of local communities and their people.

To prevent the state from financing its activities through debt, it is important to introduce an article into the constitution that makes it very difficult for the state to secure any loans. Neither should the state of the future offer any guarantees to local communities or associations of communities. Only if the possibility exists that a community may go bankrupt and find existence threatened will the large majority of the voters support a long-term solid fiscal policy at community level. The danger of bankruptcy will also force creditors to follow a prudent and responsible loan policy toward communities. Up to now, in a number of states, companies and banks have sold extravagant projects and loans to respected but inexperienced councilors, knowing that in the last resort the state will have to pay.

Only in this way will the state become a well-managed and solid service company run for the benefit of the people. What has been achieved by the state of Liechtenstein—originally a very poor state without natural resources but now without debts—should also be possible, with a solid fiscal policy, for other developed states.

A state without debt, with foreign policy and the maintenance of the rule of law as its primary duties, would become a lean and transparent state, which could be financed by a small percentage of the gross domestic product. The surplus from the revenues of indirect taxation would flow directly to local communities, which would have the authority to impose direct taxes—on companies and individuals, real estate, dogs, cats, or whatever local politicians choose. In principle, a community could also impose a tax on certain products or services in addition to the state's indirect tax. For example, to reduce consumption for health reasons, a community might levy an additional tax on alcohol or tobacco. A market economy will always ensure that those tax rates will not increase beyond a certain limit.

With the state's financial subsidies from indirect taxation and authority over direct taxation, communities should be able even with limited resources to support a basic welfare and school system, especially if the educational system is mainly financed by the state through vouchers. The financial burden of the pension system can be reduced by raising the retirement age and by encouraging private pension systems. Nevertheless, this depends on employment levels and economic development. Such a fundamental reorganization of the state should ease the financial burden on private business, give a new impetus to private consumption, accelerate the growth of the economy, and therefore increase the demand for labor. This would especially be the case for local communities that structure direct taxation and social programs in order to make it attractive again for people to work and for companies to hire additional labor.

The fear that different communities will compete to have the lowest tax rate is unfounded. The example of Switzerland and Liechtenstein shows that different tax rates between communities lead to only limited migration of companies and people from communities with higher tax rates to those with lower tax rates. Tax rates are just one of many reasons that people and companies settle where they do. For companies, other reasons are more important, such as the availability of a work force, a well-developed infrastructure, or the proximity to markets. For most people, the proximity of the work place or good schools for their children are usually more important factors than tax rates in choosing where to live. A community with high taxation and bad service will lose people and companies in the long term. In a direct democracy, it will be up to citizens to decide how attractive their community should be for people and companies.

The state of the future will offer its people much more freedom to shape the future for themselves and their descendants. Some communities will impose higher taxes but will offer better services. Others will shape their services according to the needs of the elderly, and others to the requirements of young families. Through taxation, social programs, school and transportation systems, cultural programs, building regulations, and the availability of building sites, communities in the state of the future will have considerable freedom to look for the best solution according to the wishes of their citizens and the characteristics of their area.

If the authority for direct taxation is transferred from the state to local communities, the state should establish a framework within which communities can raise taxes. Without such a framework, different communities, like states, would have to conclude tax treaties among themselves. This would overburden most communities and lead to unnecessary complications. Within that framework, each community should be free to decide the type and rate of taxation. A large community, such as a city, would probably have its own tax administration, while smaller communities would combine their tax administration or transfer it to third parties.

A favorable tax framework depends on tax competition among local communities and states. The more competition the better it is for the citizen and the taxpayer. Tax competition does not ruin the state and society; it ruins the politician who tries to "buy" votes with taxpayers' money.

One issue related to public finances, which has been the cause of many wars throughout human history, is that of mineral rights. Should mineral rights be owned by the state, local communities, or individual landowners? State ownership of mineral rights in the state of the future could lead communities with mineral resources of commercial value to secede from the state. Equally the local community in the state of the future should not own and manage mineral rights; it has enough responsibilities and should not be burdened with tasks that can be better handled by private business. Mineral rights should belong to the individual landowner.

The United States is one example where, in principle, the landowner is entitled to mineral rights. There, however, the landowner can separate his mineral rights from the ownership of the land and sell parts or all of them. This regulation has not seriously restricted the development of the mining industry in the United States, but it is probably not the best solution. Very often mineral rights were sold decades ago or have been resold and split, leading to complicated situations. Land can also be sold, resold, split, or inherited. If after many years a company finally wants to mine the minerals, it is faced with a complicated ownership situation, and equally the landowner might face an unpleasant surprise.

Much can be said in favor of keeping ownership of land and mineral rights together. The state can still establish a legal framework that takes into account the interests of affected communities and neighboring landowners, for example in the areas of water rights, the environment, or landscape protection. Communities with authority for direct taxation will also benefit from taxing both the landowner and the mining company when the minerals are extracted. The local community and its citizens will have to decide whether they value additional jobs and tax revenues more than possible damage to the environment.

A strict advocate of private ownership might argue that this proposal gives the state and local communities too much influence. However, in the state of the future, it would not be possible to extract minerals in the face of strong opposition from the local community, because the community might secede from the state and take over ownership of the mineral rights. It would also still be a better system than allowing mineral rights to be simply owned by the state, which is the case in most states today.

States that now receive most of their revenue from the extraction of minerals or from oil and gas will probably oppose the privatization of mineral rights. Nevertheless, those states must realize that, sooner or later, they will have to finance their expenses from tax revenues like other states. One day, the minerals will be exhausted, or an unforeseen technological revolution will make the further extraction of minerals unprofitable. The sooner those states prepare for this the better. Otherwise, those states might one day disappear with the exhaustion of their minerals, as have other states whose wealth was completely dependent on mineral extraction.

The state might still continue to be the best owner of mineral rights under the sea within its territorial waters or the area of continental shelf allocated to it. But even then the state will have to take into account the interests of local communities, which otherwise could leave the state and directly assume ownership of the mineral rights.

10.6 The national currency

One source of income that states have used repeatedly to finance their expenses is the monopoly over the production of money. The invention of money made trade substantially easier. The owner of a herd of cows who wanted to trade three cows for two horses no longer had to find the owner of a herd of horses who was willing to trade with him. He could instead sell his three cows to a cattle trader, and with the money he received buy his horses either from the owner of the horses or from a horse dealer. For money to be generally accepted, it must have a recognized value; moreover, it has to be easy to transport and store over long periods of time without losing its value. Initially, precious metals like gold, silver, or copper were generally used. Metals were more convenient than precious stones because they could be divided into small units or melted again into large units without any loss of value.

Over 2,000 years ago, rulers minted coins for their state territory with the metal value shown on the coin. The temptation for the ruler or the state was always to reduce the metal value of the coin but keep the nominal value on the coin and thus deceive the people. With some effort, it was possible to check the metal value of the coin and, if the difference between the metal value and the nominal value of the coin became too large, the people lost confidence in these coins. When this happened they either returned to bartering or accepted only other more valuable coins. Today, an equivalent situation would be when a weak currency is replaced by a strong one, such as when the dollar or Deutsche Mark more or less replaced the worthless national currencies of the former socialist states of Eastern Europe.

As long as state control over the population was weak and competition from neighboring states with solid currencies was strong, it was difficult for individual states to finance themselves in the long term by minting worthless coins. The growth of the money supply in a state was closely linked to the real growth of the economy. Periods of currency depreciation and inflation were relatively short and often the consequence of wars or the inflow of large quantities of precious metals. A well-known example in currency history was the large inflow of gold and silver following the discovery of the Americas, which triggered inflation especially in Spain but also in the rest of Europe. A new balance was usually found quite soon afterwards within a free market.

The Chinese Empire achieved early success in replacing a metal currency with a paper currency where the material itself lacked intrinsic value. It probably made this transition much earlier than Europe because there were no serious competitors in the immediate neighborhood; the weak Chinese paper money could not be replaced with a strong metal currency. Several attempts to replace metal currencies with paper currencies in Europe during the 17th and 18th centuries failed. Nevertheless, paper money slowly replaced metal currencies, but only as a result of the obligation to exchange paper money for gold. The increased influence of the nation-state on its citizens during the 19th century, the establishment of national banks, the unification of national economic areas, and their protection through tariffs and various other regulations made it possible for European nation-states to finance the First World War to a large extent with paper money. There were massive increases in taxation, which often included the introduction of a general income tax. The result was high inflation and a loss of public confidence in their currency. In order to restore confidence and reduce the inflation rate, a number of states decided to back their national currency formally with gold, but in reality citizens could not exchange paper money for gold. Moreover, severe currency regulations prevented competition between the individual paper currencies of Europe. By the end of the 20th century, all currencies had been detached from their metal value.

One might ask whether in a globalized world economy a state has any real need for a national currency and a national bank. Theoretically, a single global currency with its value covered by metal stocks would be the best solution in a world economy, insofar as this currency would be issued by an independent currency bank dedicated to maintaining the stable value of the currency. World trade would not be burdened by the costs of currency fluctuations and all the other risks linked to a worthless paper currency. In practice, however, a state will probably have to face the risks of a paper currency for a long time and accept the fact that the money supply in individual states will be exposed to strong fluctuations.

In principle, the state has three possibilities for protecting itself against such fluctuations, if one assumes that a national paper currency will only increase costs and risks for the national economy.

One possibility would be for the state to adopt the currency of another state whose risks are low because of the size of the state, the credibility of its national bank and statutory bodies, the lack of any limiting currency regulation, and other factors. For the small state of Liechtenstein in the 19th century, it was advantageous to introduce the crown currency of the Austro-Hungarian Empire. However, this currency collapsed during the First World War. After the war, the crown currency was replaced in Liechtenstein by the Swiss currency. The Swiss franc has the advantage of being stable and fully convertible, which means it can always be changed without restrictions into other currencies. In addition, the Swiss franc is, due to its past history, a kind of international reserve currency, so for this relatively small currency area interest rates are lower than for other currencies. Typically, interest rates are higher for currencies of small states than for larger currencies because of greater fluctuations in the currency. It is easier for speculators to force a currency to appreciate or depreciate when the currency is smaller in volume. For this reason, other small states have decided to adopt the US dollar. In the EU most member states have adopted the euro, which has become the most important currency worldwide beside the US dollar.

A second possibility would be for a state to admit all fully convertible currencies and let citizens decide which currency they want to use. In such a case a state would probably declare which currency had to be used to pay taxes and duties and in which currency it would make its payments. Local communities would also have to specify the currency payments should be made. This would constitute a return to free competition between currencies. In such a case, it might well be that, sooner or later, metal currencies would be reintroduced.

The third possibility, which I would like to examine in more detail because it is somewhat more complicated, would be a return to a metal currency. Such a solution could offer even a small state the possibility of issuing its own currency, without exposing itself to the risks of a paper currency. Small states like to have their own currency, either to be independent of the money supply of other states or for reasons of national pride.

I developed this alternative at a time when the Principality of Liechtenstein was already using the Swiss franc but did not yet have a currency treaty with Switzerland, and when Switzerland declared Liechtenstein a non-domestic currency area during a currency crisis at the beginning of the 1970s. Switzerland restricted the use of the Swiss franc for foreigners including Liechtenstein citizens. In 1980 Liechtenstein was able to conclude a currency treaty with Switzerland, and I did not pursue my plans for a metal currency in Liechtenstein any further.

It is a major advantage for a state economy to have stable exchange rates with the currencies of its most important trade partners. The higher the fluctuations in the exchange rate, the larger the risks for the importer and exporter of goods and services. Such risks can be covered to a certain degree by transactions in future markets, but these carry expenses. In any case, importers and exporters must allow for higher trading margins. The economy of a small state is much more dependent on foreign trade than the economy of a large state, and fluctuations in the exchange rate therefore influence the cost base to a larger degree.

The old metal currencies had an advantage because the national bank could fix the exchange rate in relation to other currencies. However, their disadvantage was the exposure to the fluctuations of world market prices for the metals used, usually gold and silver. The weight of the coin was fixed, as was its gold or silver content. Whenever the price of gold and silver was higher than the value of the coin, it was financially worthwhile for a speculator to buy those coins, melt them down, and then sell the gold or silver. This game could be played until the national bank had used up its gold and silver reserves.

That is essentially what happened to the US Federal Reserve Board with the US dollar, which was in a sense the only metal currency of importance until 1971. The United States made the commitment to other national banks to exchange the US dollar for gold at a price of US$35 per ounce. For American citizens the dollar had been a simple paper currency since 1933. The Federal Reserve Board allowed a much greater increase in the supply of US dollars than its gold reserves justified, resulting in a loss of confidence in the US dollar. In addition the price of gold on the free market rose far higher than US$35 per ounce. Foreign national banks started to exchange their dollars for gold at the rate of US$35 per ounce, until the Federal Reserve Board finally had to sever the link between the dollar and gold.

In a world of paper money, a small state is even less able than the United States to afford a metal currency with a guaranteed, fixed metal price, be it gold, silver, or copper. Another solution is therefore needed, which I would like to explain using a fictitious example. At one point in the 19th century, before it began to use the crown currency of the Austro-Hungarian Empire, the Principality of Liechtenstein issued its own thaler currency. What might happen today if we decided to build on this tradition of having our own currency? Depending on their value, the coins would contain gold, silver, or copper. The value of the Liechtenstein thaler in relation to other currencies would be set regularly by the Liechtenstein National Bank, according to a currency basket that would reflect the fully convertible currencies of our most important trading partners. For the Principality of Liechtenstein the most important trading partner is the euro zone, followed by the US dollar and the Swiss franc. The Liechtenstein National Bank could, for instance, fix the exchange rate of one Liechtenstein thaler to 10 euros. If the exchange rate between the Liechtenstein thaler and the euro was fixed, the metal value of the Liechtenstein thaler coins would change according to the fluctuations of the metal prices of gold, silver, and copper.

Naturally, it is not possible to adapt the metal value of all coins after they have been issued to the daily fluctuations of metal prices on the world markets. However, the metal value of the coins on the day they are minted could be adapted to prices on the world markets. To cover the cost and to make a profit, the Liechtenstein National Bank would set a fixed difference between the metal value and the nominal value of the coins. If the difference between the nominal and the metal value were 10 percent, the buyer of a Liechtenstein thaler would have to pay 10 euros. On the day when the coin was minted, the metal value would be 9 euros. The number of coins minted per day and their corresponding metal value would have to be continuously checked and published in order to prevent any misuse and to build up confidence in the new metal currency. The size of the coin could remain unchanged, but the metal value would be altered by means of changes in the alloying of the different metals, for instance gold and silver. Besides the usual information the coin would also bear the date when it was minted and perhaps a continuous numbering of the individual coins minted per day.

If a 100 thaler gold coin (assuming an exchange rate of one thaler to 10 euros) was to have a metal value of 900 euros on the day it was minted and issued, and if the metal value of the coin rose to 1,100 euros because the price of gold had increased, the owner of the coin would be able to sell his coin to a trader for the metal value and make a profit of 100 euros. If the price of gold were to fall by 200 euros and the metal value of the 100 thaler gold coin was only 700 euros, the owner of the coin would still be able to sell his coin for the fixed price of 1,000 euros to the Liechtenstein National Bank. Of course, he would then receive only paper money without any metal value, which could become a waste disposal problem if the euro were to fall to the value of the paper on which it was printed.

As can be seen, in these circumstances the currency risk for the buyer of Liechtenstein metal currency would be very low. He could always ask to be paid in Liechtenstein thalers, which would have a high metal value compared to the paper money of other currencies. The question that arises, of course, is whether the Liechtenstein National Board could face insolvency as did the US Federal Reserve Bank in 1971.

By selling the coins the Liechtenstein National Bank would make a profit of 9 percent, if we assume that the production costs for those coins are around 1 percent. By selling the 100 thaler gold coin, the Liechtenstein National Bank would receive 1,000 euros and make a book profit of around 90 euros. The Liechtenstein National Bank could invest those 1,000 euros for interest and thus earn additional profits until the owner of the 100 thaler gold coin decided to exchange his 1,000 euros again at the Liechtenstein National Bank. If in the meantime the metal value of the 100 thaler coin had fallen to 700 euros, the Liechtenstein National Bank would have to register a book loss of 210 euros less the interest earned. However, if the Liechtenstein National Bank had enough euros, it would not melt down the 100 thaler gold coin and sell the gold at a loss, but keep the coin until it could be traded again for 1,000 euros or some other convertible currency, if the demand for Liechtenstein thalers were to rise again. As a result, a great variety of coins with different metal values would be in circulation. Most coin owners would not bother to sort the coins according to their date and nominal value in order to check their metal content and then either melt down those with a higher metal value or exchange those with a lower metal value for another currency. Furthermore, the volume of coins and banknotes is usually quite stable and in most developed economies constitutes a small part of the total money supply: most of this consists of electronic money, in which nearly all payment transactions are handled.

If the Liechtenstein National Bank issued Liechtenstein thalers in the form of electronic money, it would receive, like other national banks, electronic currencies or foreign exchange, be they euros, US dollars, or Swiss francs, which it could invest in the market to earn interest. In this respect, the Liechtenstein National Bank would in principle not be much different from other national banks. Nevertheless, the Liechtenstein National Bank would be obliged by law to cover 100 percent of its own currency either with foreign exchange in another fully convertible currency or with the metal value of its own coins. The Liechtenstein National Bank would only be allowed to invest its foreign exchange with first-class banks and would be prohibited from offering loans to the public authorities in Liechtenstein.

In order to guarantee the political independence of a Liechtenstein National Bank, neither the state nor local communities would be allowed to own any shares. The state would lay down the general operating conditions and would supervise the National Bank but not run it. Only private individuals or private companies would be allowed to own shares in the National Bank. Profits would only be paid out from interest payments after the capital and the reserves had reached a certain percentage of the total money supply. The bank could not pay out the book profits realized by selling the coins because there would be at least a theoretical obligation to buy back the coins at their nominal value.

Under such conditions, a small state could easily have its own currency, which would be both stable and enjoy strong international confidence. Over time, such a currency could even develop into an international reserve currency like the Swiss franc, with the advantage of low interest rates.

As mentioned above, in a globalized world economy a single currency based on metal would probably be the best solution. However, such a solution lies in the distant future and today an "international currency bank" would probably be dependent on the governments of the different states with all the concomitant risks. In the foreseeable future, the competition between different currencies and monetary blocs offers humanity a higher degree of liberty and more protection against possible abuse from politicians than a theoretically better system with lower costs for the world economy. Unfortunately, history offers plenty of examples of new systems that seemed to be more economical at first glance but turned out to be more expensive in the long run because they placed restrictions on freedom. The merger of political units, be they communities, cantons, federal states, or states, has often been suggested as a cost-cutting measure: however, in the event they have resulted in many times more civil servants and higher expenses than before. The merger erased the competition between political units and also weakened citizens' control over politicians and the civil service.

Currency problems usually affect the financial services industry and vice versa. In 2008 the financial services industry was shaken by one of its periodic crises. In a globalized world economy a financial crisis in one state can hurt not only the national but also the international economy. As national banks and states have to play an important role in such a crisis, a few remarks might be appropriate in this context.

When I started to reorganize and rebuild the family business—which had been losing money for many years—a key element was the reorganization of a small local bank in Liechtenstein. The bank had been founded by a group of private investors after the First World War and in 1929 had to be saved from bankruptcy by the then Reigning Prince. After the Second World War, the bank was used to finance the rest of the family business and was therefore in bad shape. With the help of a good team, over the last forty years I have been able to stabilize the bank and expand it. It is now a very solid and profitable private bank active not only within but also outside Europe.

I was also involved in liberalizing the laws regulating the banking and financial services industry in Liechtenstein. Before liberalization only three banks were allowed to operate in Liechtenstein: the state bank, the Liechtensteinische Landesbank (LLB); a private bank, Verwaltungs- und Privatbank (VPB); and our own private bank, the Liechtenstein Global Trust (LGT). After liberalization, twelve additional banks were set up. None of these fifteen banks got in trouble and had to be rescued either in the 2008 crisis or in previous crises that have affected the financial services industry.

One might ask why a small financial center survived all those financial crises much better, and without government help, than much larger financial centers. One reason is certainly that the Liechtenstein banks were less involved in investment banking activities or in highly elaborate real estate projects. Perhaps more important have been Liechtenstein's laws regulating the banking and financial services industry and the quality of their supervision.

The financial crisis of 2008 has again shown that in a number of important financial centers the quality of laws and regulations was deficient, and banking supervision was inadequate. What has been said in Chapter 10.1 on the constitutional state applies also to the responsibility of state authorities toward the financial services industry. Laws and regulations have to be simple and easy to understand; otherwise, they are open to all kind of interpretations. Loopholes emerge that sooner or later will be exploited in a competitive environment. This gives opportunities to shady or incompetent players in the financial services industry and makes it more difficult to supervise this vital sector of the modern economy. The financial services industry is a sector which by its very nature is abstract and complicated.

One loophole has always been that some assets and liabilities do not show up on the balance sheet. This lack of transparency dramatically increases insecurity in a financial crisis. Assets should be shown at cost or below cost if the market price is lower. If the market price is higher, this should be mentioned in a footnote to the balance sheet but should not increase the profit that is paid out. High evaluations based on narrow or nontransparent markets have caused financial crises in the past and will cause them in the future if the problem is not addressed. Even liabilities can now be adjusted to a market price. If a rating agency downgrades a company, the liabilities of the company are reduced on the balance sheet.

A serious crisis in the financial services industry, which then spreads into the rest of the economy, usually starts with a liquidity or solvency problem in one of its major players. This can be a large bank or another large financial institution. Laws, regulation, and supervision should, therefore, focus mainly on the liquidity and solvency of large financial institutions.

The liquidity problem is easier to solve. The state or an institution such as the national bank can extend a credit line secured by the assets of the financial institution itself. The conditions under which the credit line is granted should be those of a prudent banker or merchant. States or state-like institutions are the trustees of the people and taxpayers, and are not private investors who have the liberty to spend their money as they like. Buying assets that have lost their value, or extending credit to financial institutions that have lost their solvency, is problematic. Quite often a state or state-like institution tries to cover up its past mistakes in regulating and supervising the financial services industry with a rescue package that is implemented in a hurry. A financial crisis is not the failure of the market but a failure of the state, its laws, its regulations, and its supervision.

How should the financial services industry be regulated and supervised? As mentioned before, the balance sheet of a financial services company has to be transparent; it must include all liabilities, show assets at cost or market price, whichever is lower; and—depending on the liquidity of its assets and liabilities—have enough liquidity at its disposal. The recent financial crisis has again shown that several sectors of the banking and insurance industries and also other branches of the financial services industry are quite risky. A company outside the financial services industry with similar risks would need a strong balance sheet with a high percentage of equity capital to obtain financing from a bank. A company with equity below 10 percent would have great difficulty obtaining a loan from a bank, at least from a prudent bank. On the other hand, nearly everybody is willing to lend money to banks that have, with few exceptions, equity capital below 10 percent if all liabilities are taken into account. It is, therefore, not surprising that there are periodic crises in the financial services industry. It is rather more surprising that they do not take place more frequently.

A bank with a liquidity problem and equity capital below 10 percent may quickly face a solvency problem because it will have to sell assets at a loss to resolve its liquidity problem. In a financial crisis, most bank assets will lose value and therefore reduce the equity capital of a bank. Depending on the liquidity and the inherent risks of the assets and liabilities, equity capital should finance well above 10 percent of the balance sheet.

Those states that had to intervene in the 2008 financial crisis did not give the impression of being well prepared for such a crisis. This fact increased insecurity in the national and global financial markets. Laws, regulation, and supervision were in bad shape, and there was no clear concept about how to proceed. Muddling through a crisis is connected with high costs for the economy and the taxpayer. Unfortunately this has been the policy of the day, and no fundamental reform is in sight.

In a globalized economy, a fundamental reform of the financial services sector requires the cooperation of the major international players: states require clear and simple laws and competent supervision, and large banks need better liquidity and much higher equity capital. It often appears that the markets, customers, and supervisors are more impressed by the absolute number of the equity capital shown on the balance sheet than by what percentage this equity capital represents in relation to total assets and liabilities. To allow less than 10 percent is irresponsible if one takes into account the financial crises of recent times; but to ask for more than 20 percent might be politically difficult, because it would reduce lending and increase interest rates over a longer period of time.

Large international banks in high risk sectors will therefore remain a systematic risk and a moral hazard for the national and global economy. They are too big to fail. Liquidity will probably not be the main issue as long as those banks have bankable assets that can either be sold or used as security for a loan. Solvency will remain the fundamental problem.

Let us assume that in the future major players like the United States, the EU, Japan, and others can agree on a new set of rules similar to those described in this chapter. Let us further assume that a large international bank, too big to fail, with a capital ratio of 18 percent, has not only a liquidity but also a solvency problem. It might lose more than half of its equity capital but would, according to present rules, still be sufficiently capitalized. Nevertheless, private investors might be unwilling to refinance such a bank. Then the states in which this bank is active and supervised will have to cooperate to rescue the bank according to a set of rules that has been previously agreed and published. The states will recapitalize the bank on terms that are attractive for them and their taxpayers, perhaps replace the management, and reorganize the bank so that the invested capital can be paid back in the foreseeable future either through the sale of shares or some other mechanism.

If the 2008 financial crisis could convince the major players that fundamental reforms are needed to prevent the next financial crisis—or at least reduce its impact—then it might at least have had some benefits. It will take a few years for the large banks and some of the other bigger companies in the financial services industry to raise their equity capital to an adequate level. The sooner this process begins, the better we will be prepared for the next financial crisis—and one will certainly come.

10.7 Other state duties

During the last two hundred years, states have taken over many other duties besides the maintenance of the rule of law and the conduct of foreign policy. These other duties are financed with taxpayers' money. One can justifiably ask whether the following tasks could not be performed more efficiently in the future by private enterprise, local communities, or regional associations of local communities: the operation of radio and television stations, postal services, telecommunications, and national cultural institutions such as museums, operas, or theatres. The example of the United States has shown that a state and its national authorities do not need to operate these services and can still have effective radio, television, telecommunications, museums and so on that are managed and financed by private enterprise—often providing better quality than the state-financed competition. In contrast the US state-run postal service was always a shining example of state incompetence. In the United States and Europe, private postal services have been able to compete successfully against the state-run postal service, and it is difficult to see why state postal services cannot be fully privatized.

Defense as part of foreign relations has traditionally been one of the main duties of the state. As mentioned in the first part of this book, wars were not an invention of the agrarian age, but have occurred from the very beginning of humanity. They have not only caused much human suffering but have been far more expensive than even the most stupid agricultural policy. Even in peacetime the military expenditure of the OECD countries exceeds their expenditure on agriculture many times over. One day, perhaps, states will become peaceful service companies, which will no longer demand that citizens sacrifice their lives for "God and the Fatherland." In order to reach this goal, states, politicians, and the people have to accept the fact that states are not gods and that people do not have to serve them or even sacrifice their life for the glory of the nation or create heaven on earth for the chosen people. In the hope that for the state of the future, wars will be a distant bad dream,

I shall not go into more details about defense policy as a state duty. In the future states should fight for their clients—the local communities and their populations—in peaceful competition on the basis of good and efficient service at an acceptable price. In Chapter 12 I shall describe possible strategies to help humanity reach this objective.

As long as a new, peaceful world order has not been realized, there will be wars. Fortunately, it seems that since the end of the Cold War the danger of a third world war or of long and large wars between states has been substantially reduced. An aggressor runs the risk that the leading military powers would help the state that is under attack and defeat the aggressor with the consent of the United Nations—as happened with the liberation of Kuwait after the Iraqi aggression.

However, in the past we have seen wars in which the great powers did not intervene, for instance, between India and Pakistan or between China and Vietnam. They were comparatively short, locally limited, and did not bring important territorial gains or decisive victories for the aggressor, with the exception of Israel's victory over its Arab neighbors in 1967. Since then, however, Israel has withdrawn from some of the occupied territories without obtaining the most important goal: a peace treaty with all its neighbors and internationally recognized boundaries.

Today, danger emanates less from conventional or nuclear wars between states than from terrorism, guerrilla warfare, or civil wars—each one potentially involving the use of weapons of mass destruction. A traditional defense policy or traditional army can hardly deal with these threats: on the contrary, they seem to aggravate those dangers and connected problems. To master these threats, what is needed is a state where the rule of law prevails, and which is able to solve political, economic, and social problems.

Foreign policy will remain one of the state's duties in its relations with other states and its membership in regional and international organizations. In a globalized world, foreign policy will become even more important as the relations among states and their people become ever closer in areas such as the economy, society, tourism, or culture. In addition to the ministry of foreign affairs and embassies, international organizations such as the UN, WTO, World Health Organization, EU, Organization of American States, Organisation of African Unity, Association of Southeast Asian Nations, and NATO are becoming more important in relations between states. In these international organizations, regular meetings take place on different levels from the heads of state down to civil servants and experts. At state level, where representatives of the executive branch are active in one way or another, these organizations are only one part of the extensive foreign affairs network that connects the states. There are regional and international organizations for the legislature and the courts, where deputies and judges are active. Below state level, networks have been created for local communities, cities, and regions that cross not only state borders but also continents.

In our globalized world, public sector networks are supplemented by networks in the private sector, such as the economy, non-governmental organizations (NGOs), culture, and tourism. Of course, a state can try to isolate all these private and public networks. We can observe the results of such a policy on the population in Eastern Europe under communism and still today in North Korea or Myanmar, the former Burma. In the long run, such a policy is bound to fail. Traditional foreign policy, as it evolved over centuries, is being fundamentally transformed by globalization. The costs of transportation and communication are falling rapidly and have led worldwide to a rapid growth of private and public networks, and this trend will continue. It is still difficult to judge what the effects of such developments will be on the traditional state and its foreign policy. In any case many world problems can only be solved by close cooperation between states.

In most developed states, foreign aid has become a part of foreign policy. As much as I am convinced that it is one of our duties to help poor people in the Third World, I am also convinced that foreign aid by rich industrial states to the Third World in its present form is usually not only useless, but often counterproductive.

A longstanding criticism of state aid to developing countries is that it involves poor taxpayers in industrial states being forced to finance rich potentates in the Third World, who then invest the money either in their private accounts or in useless projects in which a few large companies from industrial states will earn a lot of money. Anyone who has followed the history of foreign aid from its beginning during decolonization approximately fifty years ago will know that state foreign aid has also been used to keep corrupt and cruel dictators and oligarchies in power. Foreign aid, yes, but not from state to state: rather it should be from private people to private people, from NGOs to the people, or from local communities to local communities; and above all it should only be offered to states that are seriously trying to build democratic constitutional states with the rule of law and a market economy integrated into the global world economy.

State foreign aid should concentrate mainly on helping the Third World to build up the rule of law and a market economy. For this task no large sums are required, but rather experienced judges, lawyers, and policemen, who are willing to spend a few years in one of those developing countries. In addition, state foreign aid could finance a system of educational vouchers as described in Chapter 10.3.

11. A constitution for the state of the future

In Chapter 10, I described what the state of the future could look like. In this chapter, I will describe the draft of a possible constitution for such a state. For reasons mentioned in Chapter 8, the constitution of Liechtenstein has served as a useful model. A constitution that has developed over decades has additional advantages, such as experience with regard to the workability of individual articles or the availability of decisions by a constitutional court that can be used to interpret the constitution. Where it made sense, the structure of the constitution with its different chapters and the wording of individual articles has therefore been maintained. Nevertheless, many articles and some chapters have been deleted or merged because they have lost their meaning since they were first adopted or are of no importance for the state of the future as described in Chapter 10. A complete draft constitution is included in the appendix to this book. This chapter serves as a commentary.

The draft constitution is phrased in such a way that it can be used for a hereditary monarchy or for a republic with an elected monarch as head of state. A draft constitution relying on the principles of self-determination, the rule of law, and direct and indirect democracy, is not significantly different whether it is for a hereditary monarchy or a republic. As a monarch, and because I give a hereditary monarchy a better chance of surviving over a long period of time, I have given precedence in my draft to the monarchy and put the republican equivalent in brackets. In order to avoid giving the reader the impression that the draft might have been written for a particular monarchy or republic, the monarchy has been named "Kingdom X" and the republic "Republic Y."

Most constitutions and many state treaties have a comprehensive introduction or preamble containing general declarations on the principles or the objectives of the constitution or the treaty. Lawyers differ about whether preambles entitle citizens to rights that they can claim in court. If the declarations in the preamble have no legal consequences, it is better to drop them. If they have legal consequences, adding to understanding of, and confidence in, the constitution, these declarations should be integrated into the actual text of the constitution. The constitution of Liechtenstein never had a preamble and this has probably spared Liechtenstein citizens a number of unnecessary court cases. Based on this experience and with the goal of formulating a constitution that is short, simple, and easy to understand, this draft constitution has no preamble.

The state, with its fundamental principles, purpose, and tasks, is defined in Chapter I, Articles 1 to 4. To prevent the state from taking over more and more tasks, Article 2, concerning the state's duties, emphasizes particularly that the state has to leave all other duties to local communities or private organizations. A clear division of duties and political responsibility between the state and local communities requires a division of the tax authority (Article 3), which has to be equally clear in order to avoid a slow erosion of autonomy and the right of self-determination at local level. The right of local communities to leave the state, as regulated in Article 4, will ensure that the state is transformed from an inefficient monopoly into an efficient service company, which offers its customers optimum service at a certain price level.

Chapter II, Articles 5 to 12, regulates the position, rights, duties, succession or appointment, and possible removal of the head of state. The removal of the head of state (Article 12) is to be decided in a republic by the constitutional court and in a monarchy, as in Liechtenstein, by the house law and the ruling house. For the election of the president of the republic (Article 5) a procedure has been chosen that should as far as possible avoid polarization within the people: such a procedure is already in force in the constitution of Liechtenstein for the selection of judges and is regulated in Article 47.

Chapter III, Articles 13 to 21, defines the rights and obligations of citizens. Compared with the Liechtenstein constitution, the number of articles has been considerably reduced: this chapter in the Liechtenstein constitution still contains a number of articles and regulations that are no longer needed in the constitution of a state in the third millennium.

Chapter IV, concerning the parliament, Articles 22 to 32, envisages twenty-five representatives, which is probably the lower limit if the experience of

Liechtenstein is considered. In a system of proportional representation with twenty-five representatives, there is a threshold clause of at least 4 percent for a party or electoral group. For the state of the future, which gives local communities a high level of autonomy, a system of proportional representation should be a better solution than a system with majority representation, which requires that the state be divided into individual constituencies. Constituencies have to be adapted geographically to a changing population, in order to prevent some individual votes becoming more important than others. In the system of proportional representation, different states have used different percentages for the threshold clause, usually between 1 and 10 percent.

In Chapter V, concerning the government, Articles 33 to 37, five members of government are envisaged, as explained in Chapter 10.1. This should be sufficient even for a large state with reduced state duties, and assuming that the state of the future will not need a minister of defense or an army. Well-trained and well-equipped police forces and the surveillance of airspace and territorial waters would be the responsibility of the ministry of the interior. As explained in Chapter 12, such units could also be used for peace missions abroad.

In connection with Chapter VI, concerning the courts, Articles 38 to 43, it should be noted that the procedures for the nomination of judges (Article 39) have turned out to be successful since their introduction in Liechtenstein in 2003. Candidates have been chosen for their professional qualities, and political considerations have been disregarded in the appointment process. Contrary to some fears, so far there has been no conflict between the selection committee for judges and parliament, and the people have not had to elect a judge. In a large state, where many judges have to be appointed, such a selection committee for judges will probably have to delegate some of its duties.

Chapter VII, Articles 44 and 45, covers two areas. Article 44 sets out the fundamental principles that govern the organization and duties of local communities; and in Article 45 public liability towards third parties is established, be it at state or community level.

Chapter VIII, Articles 46 and 47, regulates the procedures for changing the constitution. Another procedure is necessary to transform a monarchy into a republic or a republic into a monarchy, so as to eliminate the monarch or president's power of veto (Article 47). Useful as the veto power of the head of state may be in a direct democracy, even if it is only rarely threatened and even more rarely applied, it must not be misused by the monarch or president for the purpose of preventing a fundamental change in the form of the state which is desired by a majority of the people.

Article 47 Paragraph 2 describes voting procedures in case the people have to choose between more than two proposals. This procedure is already established in the constitution of Liechtenstein. The same procedure is envisaged for the election of the president in the republic (Article 5) and for the election of judges (Article 39, Paragraph 2), if the people have to choose between more than two candidates. This procedure is designed to prevent the elimination in the first round of a proposal or candidate that might be the second-best solution for a majority of the people, if the preferred solution does not receive enough votes. In a vote between more than two proposals or candidates, other voting procedures can mean that a compromise solution does not reach the second round because in the first round everybody has voted for the solution he likes best. As a result, very often two extreme proposals reach the second round of voting and divide the people more than a possible compromise. The same problem arises if there is only one round of voting and the relative majority decides.

The final provisions are included in Chapter IX, Article 48. They correspond to the provisions of the Liechtenstein constitution and give the constitutional court the authority to revoke or declare invalid all laws, decrees, and statutory provisions that contradict the new constitution.

The proposed draft constitution for the state in the third millennium could also be the basis for an alternative to the much discussed, but now rejected, draft constitution of the EU. It would be shorter and easier to understand and would therefore have a better chance of being accepted in a popular vote.

Such a constitution for the EU would eliminate the current highly complicated and inefficient financial arrangements such as subsidies for agriculture, and the manifold subsidies for states, regions, and projects, as well as individual rebates to states. The financial redistribution between richer and poorer regions inside the EU would be realized through value added tax as described in Chapter 10.5, which would be simpler, fairer, and more transparent.

Additional changes would, of course, be necessary for the draft EU constitution. States would take the place of local communities. The distribution of duties, the authority to make laws, and the justice system would also have to be regulated in a different way. Should the member states of the EU introduce within their borders the right of self-determination at local community level and direct democracy as described in the draft constitution, an incredibly dynamic Europe could be created. It would be an example for the rest of the world.

In the case of the EU, the republican model would probably be the right choice, since the majority of EU member states are republics, and even those that are monarchies would be unlikely to accept the idea that one of the reigning houses should be given a preferred position. Even though the English monarchy has a privileged position, based on its history and the importance of Great Britain both inside and outside the EU, it is doubtful whether even the British people would wish to give their royal house a politically stronger position inside the EU than in their own country. Ideally the citizens of the EU could decide whether they would prefer a monarchy or a republican model. If the citizens were to vote for a monarchy they would then have to decide in a second vote which family should provide the monarch. If the citizens voted for a republic they would have to decide every four years which citizen of the EU should become president.

12. Strategies to achieve the state of the future

It is entertaining and intellectually satisfying to criticize existing systems and to design better ones. In order to realize better systems one needs a strategy or sometimes several strategies to move from inferior system A to superior system B. It is necessary to take into account the fact that many people are prisoners of the present system and are fearful to change it because such a change may carry unforeseeable risks.

Despite my criticisms of politicians, the reader should not forget that those politicians are even more the prisoners of the present political system than other citizens. They have grown up in this system and made their political careers there, and if they turn against their political system, they are usually expelled by it. Only in a few cases, usually during a political crisis, can a politician or a group of politicians make fundamental changes to the system. My family, too, has been and still is today part of this political system. We provide the monarch for the small Principality of Liechtenstein; we were part of the political oligarchy of the Holy Roman Empire; and later, we remained, in one form or another, part of the oligarchic network of Europe.

At least two strategies are needed to realize the states of the future. The first strategy would be open to existing democratic constitutional states, where the people have some influence on the future of their state, at least indirectly by electing the parliament. The second strategy would be appropriate for those states where the people have no influence on the future of their states through elections.

The strategy for democratic states is simple, at least in theory. First, it is necessary to convince the majority of the people that it is necessary to reform the political structures of the state, and then the elected politicians will carry out the wishes of the people. In reality, of course, this is not so simple. In most cases people are not very interested in politics, and the willingness of politicians to fulfill the wishes of the people is limited.

The present system of indirect democracy offers the political oligarchy advantages that they might lose, fully or in part, if the improvements proposed in this book were to be implemented. As in the case of the old aristocracy, the political oligarchy of today usually ensures that the political oligarch who has lost his job and his power will not lose all his privileges. In the old days, family networks inside the nobility took care of that, but today it is the network of the political parties that takes over this task. Without direct democracy and the right of self-determination at local community level, indirect democracy remains a controlled democracy ruled by an oligarchy which has replaced the mantle of religious legitimation with the mantle of democratic legitimation. In elections the people can only choose between a black, red, green, or blue mantle. If no party receives an absolute majority, the oligarchy of the parties will decide on the color combination. The smaller the ideological differences between the parties and the more pragmatic their oligarchies, the easier it is to combine the different colors. As in the old days of aristocratic rule, one of the main purposes is to keep power and privilege within the party oligarchies.

Nevertheless, the study of history provides examples of citizens suddenly becoming intensely interested in political problems and bringing about a change in the political system. In such a case, it is an advantage if a new constitutional concept has already been worked out and can be discussed. I hope this book would make a small contribution, should such a situation present itself in one or another state in the future. The discussion should first focus on the question of direct democracy. Anyone who rejects direct democracy will also reject the proposed model for the state in the third millennium, because without direct democracy it will hardly be possible to turn the old state into a service company for the people.

Not only politicians, but also sections of the population, might reject direct democracy out of the honest conviction that the majority has neither the intellectual nor the moral ability to decide about the future of the state, and that such decisions are therefore better left to an oligarchy or to a monarch, whether elected or not. Such an opinion must be respected, but logically those people should also then reject indirect democracy. Experience shows that it is usually much easier to make a decision on questions of fact than on personnel matters, especially if this personnel decision relates to a politician whom one hardly knows and a party program that might consist mostly of empty promises. Anyone who believes that the average citizen lacks the intelligence to decide an increase or decrease in taxation which affects him directly should not burden the same citizen with indirect democracy. What is then left is an enlightened absolutism, where the monarchs or presidents and oligarchs decide for the good of the people. It is doubtful whether this would be a credible party program for winning elections in indirect democracies in the long term.

Those people who are convinced about the advantages of direct democracy should first try to convince politicians to change the constitution, so that the people obtain the right of direct democracy in those states which currently only have indirect democracy. This is basically the case in all democratic states with the exception of Switzerland and Liechtenstein. However, this is not easy. Leading politicians are skeptical about strengthening direct democracy, even in states which already have it. This is understandable because direct democracy reduces the political power of leading politicians in a state based on oligarchic rule.

The supporters of direct democracy will have to consider establishing their own party if the resistance in the existing parties is too strong. To establish a new party is quite difficult in most states and requires time, money, and considerable patience. However, it is neither likely nor necessary that a newly established party will become a majority party within a short period of time. It is sufficient to prove to the existing parties that there are enough voters who want to have more democracy. The green parties, which have been formed in many states, are a good example. For a long time, environmental issues were of little interest to the old parties until a relatively small proportion of votes cast for the green parties led to a reconsideration of the matter. The influence of green parties, even if they are small and not represented in the government, extends well beyond the boundaries of their own parties and far beyond their size.

Apart from working with political parties, working with the media is also important. The media should be natural allies of direct democracy. Direct democracy gives the media the opportunity to raise political questions, discuss solutions to problems, and even implement them by popular vote.

The reader may be astonished that up to now the media have not been addressed in this book, despite the fact that they play such an important role in a democratic constitutional state. The main reason is that the state in the future should not be involved in the media. State radio and television or state subsidies to the media give politicians the possibility of influencing the media. The state should restrict itself to laying down the legal framework within which the media are able to work. This includes the protection of the private sphere of the individual and the right to demand corrections of false announcements, which must be published within a reasonable time frame and to a reasonable extent.

Criticism of many media for their low intellectual and moral content is certainly justified, but the media are the mirror of our society. The media report in essence what the public wants to read, to hear, and to see: sensations, entertainment, gossip, sex, and crime. We have to come to terms with the fact that most media provide entertainment and not information. Unfortunately, there are media that intentionally publish false reports if it suits their purpose, often for political and commercial reasons. Without engaging in long court cases, it is often difficult to obtain a correction from the media, as I know from personal experience as the victim of such false announcements. This somewhat sad situation is, nevertheless, still better than if the media were under the strict control of the state and the politicians. Direct democracy and political decentralization might lead to a higher diversity in the media landscape. At least in Switzerland and Liechtenstein, there is a higher diversity than in states that are much larger but have only indirect democracy and political centralization.

Political development in democratic states over the last few decades has shown that direct democracy has gained ground very slowly, but steadily. It seems that people want to have more democracy, and politicians cannot completely avoid this trend, even if they are usually successful in restricting direct democracy. The strengthening of this trend towards more direct democracy will be the task of all democrats in close cooperation with politicians, parties, and the media.

It only makes sense to take the next step towards the realization of the state of the future when this first battle over direct democracy has been won. This book can only sketch what the state of the future should look like. States willing to take such a step will need to assemble a team of experts with different backgrounds, who will work out a constitution that respects local wishes and traditions. States and people are different. What has worked well in one state might not be the best solution in another. The people of the Principality of Liechtenstein want a hereditary monarchy, but the people of our neighbor

Switzerland want a republic. When I established the Liechtenstein Institute on Self-Determination at Princeton University in 2000, it was with the hope that sometime in the future this institute might be in a position to offer advice whenever such concepts are developed. Already today, under the leadership of Professor Wolfgang Danspeckgruber, the institute has an excellent group of faculty and members and an international network of renowned experts, from different continents and cultures, who could be helpful in such projects.

Not only has a constitution to be worked out for the state in the third millennium: laws have to be adapted for the different legal and administrative dimensions. Many laws which are already well proven in various states can be adopted with small changes, while others will have to be rewritten. The Liechtenstein Institute on Self-Determination could work out drafts with its faculty, students, and international network of experts. The institute would welcome ideas regarding the state concept or the draft constitution as well as the drafts of the individual laws discussed in this book (Liechtenstein Institute on Self-Determination, Bendheim Hall, Princeton, New Jersey 08544, USA; email: lisd@princeton.edu).

A democratic constitutional state has at its disposal most of the rules through which it can be transformed peacefully and without revolution into a service company that serves the people and not the politicians. It is more difficult in those states that do not have those democratic rules or in states where such rules are not worth the paper on which they are written and which call themselves democratic constitutional states only because it is expedient to do so. The German Democratic Republic, for example, called itself a democracy, but it was a prison. When the door of that prison opened, the people started to flee from the self-appointed workers' and farmers' paradise.

In the past the behavior of democratic states towards dictatorships was often guided by political realism or opportunism. In a number of cases the most serious violations of human rights did not disturb the close cooperation with those states; on the contrary, they were often denied or played down. Left-wing politicians and media kept silent about violations committed by left-leaning dictatorships, and those on the right were silent about dictatorships of the political right. There were military interventions against a number of dictatorships by democratic constitutional states only after those dictatorships attacked other states, for instance, the war against the Third Reich under Hitler or against Iraq under Saddam Hussein. There have also been a number of military interventions against dictatorships in cases of serious violations of human rights such as the murder or expulsion of large groups of the population, for instance, in the former Yugoslavia. In a number of other cases where a military intervention would have been feasible, the democratic constitutional states stood by and watched, especially in Africa, or waited so long that it was no longer possible to save thousands of innocent people.

It should also be remembered that the United States intervened militarily in Latin America again and again before and after the Second World War, usually with the aim of toppling a dictatorship and introducing indirect democracy according to the American model. Nearly all these attempts failed miserably, and some corrupt oligarchies and dictators resumed power.

In cases of serious violations of human rights or of genocide, democratic constitutional states have to determine when one stands by and does nothing and when one intervenes. In a globalized and electronically integrated world with a multitude of personal contacts from tourism, trade, the service industry, etc., it is becoming increasingly difficult for politicians in democratic constitutional states to stand by and do nothing. Seventy years ago, it was still possible to send back Jewish refugees whose lives were threatened in their home country. Today, refugees can still be sent back to Africa or Asia. The question is: for how long? On the one hand, the pressure of public opinion to save those people will become stronger and stronger because of the global integration of the media and the many personal relationships in a globalized world. On the other hand, there has not been a successful recipe up to now for turning a dictatorship into a democratic, constitutional, and economically successful state by military intervention.

The successful transformation of Germany and Japan after the Second World War into democratic constitutional states with indirect democracy and a successful market economy was mainly the famous exception that proves the rule. It is easy to overlook the fact that Germany and Japan had been constitutional states with indirect democracy and a more or less successful market economy until the world economic crisis, when national socialism and nationalism took over. The world economic crisis of 1929 triggered a nationalistic wave that engulfed economic sense in a protectionist sea. International trade collapsed, and the economic crisis became worse. Among the large states, Germany and Japan were specially hit because they had, relatively speaking, few natural resources and were more dependent on trade than other large states. They had no colonial empires, and a nationalistic ideology demanded wars of conquest in order to become independent of trade.

After their military victory, the allies more or less restored the political situation in Germany and Japan as it had been before the nationalistic dictatorships took over. Unfortunately, subsequent military interventions and the whole process of decolonialization were, with few exceptions, less successful. Sooner or later, corrupt dictators and oligarchies again came to power and destroyed the democratic constitutional state and the market economy with promises to realize heaven on earth through nationalistic and socialistic ideologies. Since the traditional democratic constitutional states had also been infected after the Second World War by nationalistic and socialistic ideologies, the same medicine was and still is prescribed, namely a state with indirect democracy that is supposed to bring heaven on earth to the people. This can be compared to a doctor who has prescribed to his patients the same medicine for decades, despite the fact that in over 90 percent of the cases the medicine is deadly and the chances of healing are less than 10 percent. Such a doctor would not only have been banned long ago from his profession, but he would face civil and perhaps even criminal charges.

Traditional democratic constitutional states have to accept that for decades their "medicine" has turned out to be deadly in most cases, but on the other hand that there will be "patients" where it is simply not possible to stand by and do nothing. If the people in democratic constitutional states watch TV coverage of the mass murder of innocent people in another state without emotion and without asking for intervention, we would have cause to worry about the situation in these constitutional states. Will the same people also stand by and do nothing in their own state, perhaps if an unpopular minority is murdered? In a globalized world we will have to take into account the fact that people in democratic constitutional states will put increasing pressure on their politicians to intervene in dictatorships where people are being expelled, oppressed, or murdered. Compassionate speeches, some prayers, and a few sanctions, which do not harm anybody, will not be sufficient in the long run. Simply to take in all the refugees is no solution either.

Ideally, democratic constitutional states should agree within the framework of the UN under what conditions a member state of the UN should be subjected to military intervention, and how it can be ensured that after such an intervention a state would emerge that is democratic, follows the rule of law, and is economically successful. Such a state will not produce political and economic refugees. However, perhaps I am too pessimistic, but it does not look as if in the foreseeable future such a concept can be worked out within the framework of the UN.

I therefore want to propose an alternative however controversial, which might have a better chance of success. I have been making politically controversial statements since I was a student and continued during my time as head of state, so I am not afraid of controversy now, after my retirement from active politics. My experience has been that controversial discussions very often produce better results than too much diplomacy. If someone produces a better solution to this problem than what I propose, then all the better.

Realistically, only the United States, as the last remaining superpower, has the military, financial, and political capability to carry out a large military intervention in a relatively short time. The United States has recently shown in Iraq that it can, under difficult circumstances, carry out a successful military intervention in a short time. From a military standpoint the allies were not needed; indeed they probably made the military intervention rather more complicated. Rapid progress in military technology might well complicate the coordination of military forces from different states. Much can, therefore, be said in favor of leaving the purely military side of such an intervention to the United States. The other democratic constitutional states can then concentrate on the transformation of such a state into a politically and economically successful state after the military intervention.

This would mean that only the US government would decide about a major military intervention; but in reality this is already the case. Nearly all democratic constitutional states which have the capability of intervening militarily in another state are more or less dependent on the United States for military technology, military intelligence, and transport capabilities. It will become increasingly difficult for a democratic constitutional state to intervene in another state against the will of the United States. As early as 1956, the United Kingdom, France, and Israel had this experience, when they occupied the Sinai and the Suez Canal. Under American pressure they had to retreat.

As it would be up to the US government to decide when, where, and how a military intervention should take place, I have refrained from wasting many words on this subject. Nevertheless, a military intervention by the United States will only be a long-term success if it is possible subsequently to establish a functioning democratic constitutional state. It is therefore advisable for the United States to reach an agreement beforehand with other democratic constitutional states about the circumstances in which a military intervention should take place and what has to happen immediately afterwards. For a dictatorship that despises human rights, such an agreement and its publication would act as a deterrent. Those dictatorships would have to reckon with a more or less automatic military intervention and the transformation of their state into a democratic constitutional state, if they violate human rights in a serious way.

There are good reasons to separate military intervention in a state such as Iraq from the other tasks. The highly mechanized American task forces are trained and equipped to eliminate as quickly as possible enemy military forces with a minimum of casualties on their own side, to gain territory, and to reach tactical and strategic goals. Even if, at the beginning, the population welcomes such an army as a liberator, historic examples have shown repeatedly that foreign military units are not equipped and trained to maintain law and order or to build a democratic constitutional state and an efficient market economy that can be integrated into the world economy. The United States, as the leading military power, should withdraw as quickly as possible after a successful military intervention, and leave those other tasks to a partner who is well prepared for them.

The EU could be the partner to take over the task of building a democratic constitutional state with a market economy. Nearly all former colonial powers are now members of the EU. Through these former colonial powers, the EU has at its disposal a diverse and extensive network in all continents. Worldwide, the EU is the largest trade bloc, and the euro is the most important currency next to the dollar. The EU has established laws for its members that also give non-members the possibility of economic integration within the framework of the European Economic Area (EEA). Instead of maintaining a multitude of smaller military forces in the individual EU states, which cost a substantial amount of money, have doubtful military value, and are more or less dependent on the United States, it would be more appropriate to set up a new type of force that would be in the position to help to transform the state in question into a democratic constitutional state immediately after a military intervention.

What should such a task force look like? It should include highly mobile police units that could maintain law and order immediately after the fighting has ended. These would require helicopters and surveillance drones in order to control large territories. They would require people who know the conditions in the area as well as the language of the local population. One unit would be needed to train or retrain the local police force. Police units which have been trained and used by a dictatorship have to be retrained if they are to be used in a democratic constitutional state. If the external security of this state is guaranteed by the United States and the other democratic constitutional states, the army of that state could be dissolved. Armies are an economic burden for those states, are often a threat to the domestic policy of a young democracy, and might be a threat to neighbors. The members of the dissolved army should have the opportunity to become members of the new police unit after adequate retraining. This would prevent soldiers who have been trained in the use of weapons from remaining unemployed and becoming a reservoir of recruits for national and international terrorist organizations.

As well as police units to keep law and order in such a state, it is necessary to have a constitution and laws that meet the standards of a democratic constitutional state. This means that even before a military intervention takes place, a new constitution for the state has to be worked out and existing laws have to be adapted. Lawyers who are citizens of this state should be retained as advisors. In many cases these will be individuals who are close to the political opposition or have been in exile. Since an opposition in exile is often deeply divided and not representative of the whole population, such individuals who are former exiles should not make the final decisions about the new constitution or the adaptation of the existing laws. Those decisions should rest with the EU or with those democratic constitutional states that have taken upon themselves the responsibility for maintaining law and order and rebuilding a democratic constitutional state. There is no reason not to publish the new constitution and the adapted laws before a decision on a military intervention has been made. On the contrary, this could increase the political pressure on the dictatorship to reform.

In a dictatorship the state has usually taken on many duties that would be undertaken in a democratic state at the community or local level or by private enterprise. The constitution and the laws should therefore correspond to the state of the future as described in this book, because it will be difficult enough for a new democratic constitutional state to maintain the rule of law and be economically successful. To achieve this, transitional regulations must be worked out. Property which has been expropriated by the state must be returned to its former owners. Where this is not possible, compensation should be paid from the proceeds of all state property that is to be privatized.

The police, the constitution, and the law are just one side of the democratic constitutional state. A constitutional state needs independent courts and well-trained judges. The EU, with its cultural and linguistic diversity, should be able to provide a team of lawyers who would be available as independent judges and as instructors for a number of years. It is especially important for such a legal team to follow closely the decisions of the highest courts. The best constitutions and laws can, intentionally or unintentionally, be deprived of their force through poor decisions by a court.

In addition to security and legal issues, the EU would have an equally important role to play in economic stabilization and development in a new democratic constitutional state. One way of promoting economic stabilization and development would be to allow the new state membership of the EEA (whose current members are the EU states, Iceland, Liechtenstein, and Norway). This would give a new democratic constitutional state free access to the whole European market and would guarantee the implementation of the economic regulations of the EU. Experts from the EU or EEA would advise and train the administration of such a state on how to implement these regulations. From an economic point of view, this would be advantageous both for the new state and for the EU. The EU would gain better access to the markets of the new state without having to grant it EU membership, which—even if it were geographically appropriate—would be politically difficult and would cost the EU much more because of high subsidies for agriculture and other areas.

The EEA offers the possibility of imaginative and flexible economic solutions. The Principality of Liechtenstein is a member of the EEA and Switzerland is not, but Liechtenstein has a customs union with Switzerland. Products that meet the specifications of the EU can be sold freely on the Liechtenstein market, but if they do not meet Swiss specifications, they cannot be exported from Liechtenstein to Switzerland. On the other hand, Swiss products that cannot be exported to the EU because they do not correspond to EU specifications can be sold without problems in Liechtenstein. To be able to sell products and services corresponding to different specifications in the same market is even more important for a member state of the EEA outside Europe than for the Principality of Liechtenstein, because regional trade with non-EU states will be more important.

How large would an EU task force need to be to carry out the role of building a democratic constitutional state? If one takes a state of the size and population of Iraq as an example, such a task force, comprising police, judges, and other experts, would probably have to consist of about 200,000 people in order to restore law and order as rapidly as possible. This would mean about ten task force personnel per 1,000 inhabitants. There are experts who say that the number should be twenty-five per 1,000: experience has shown, however, that task forces with fewer than ten members per 1,000 inhabitants have also been successful. Success is probably less dependent on numbers than on the political goals of the intervention, the strategy followed, the leadership, the training and equipment of the total task force, and, of course, the terrain. However, at the beginning it is better to err on the high side than, as in Iraq, on the low side.

The police would be by far the largest unit in such a task force. However, this number could be reduced rapidly as soon as local police units were available. How long the other experts would have to remain would depend on how long it would take to build an economically successful, democratic constitutional state. The courts might also have to deal with the difficult problem of judging possible crimes by the old dictatorship. Much tact and sensitivity would be needed to avoid opening old sores, inspiring acts of revenge, and turning criminals into martyrs. In such a situation the local population would probably have more confidence in the objectivity of foreign judges than in the judges of the old regime.

If such a task force of about 200,000 members is compared with the much larger and more expensive military forces of the EU member states, it is clear that the task force would be a smaller burden from a financial and human perspective but would have a much more positive influence in the world today. The costs could be further reduced if members of this EU-led task force were mainly recruited from the Third World. An additional advantage would be that people from Third World countries would receive good training that would be useful when they returned home. The task force would have an international makeup, if possible recruited mainly from the regions in which they would be most likely to be deployed. Its language would have to be English, not least because of the close cooperation that would be necessary with the United States. As the task force would be active in different regions, language skills are important: ideally, each member of the task force should speak at least one other language besides English.

What would have been different, taking Iraq as an example, if such a task force had been available? Years before the intervention a new constitution for Iraq could have been worked out and laws adapted; furthermore, all this could have been published. Refugees from Iraq could have been recruited and trained as policemen, judges, and lawyers. At the beginning of the military intervention, the EU task force could have taken over areas liberated by American military forces and introduced law and order. The population could have been informed by the media and leaflets about their rights and duties, including those concerning the military forces of the United States and the police forces of the EU.

If the EU wants to set up a democratic state, it should grant the population the same rights as its own population in order to prevent unauthorized acts on the part of police units and the US army. In areas controlled by the EU police units, the population could be registered and given forgery-proof identity cards with the usual personal information, including residential address; and when the fighting ends, at the earliest possible date, local elections should take place in reasonably safe areas. Such local elections are important as a first step because a stable and working democracy has to be built from the bottom up, particularly in a state that has never been a working democratic constitutional state or where a dictatorship has destroyed those structures. Through local elections, the EU would gain partners who would enjoy the support of the population. If one tries to build a democracy from the top down, by having first a general election for a parliament or a constitutional convention, this gives the old or the new oligarchy the chance to take over political power. Then the state will not serve the people but will serve the oligarchy, and, in the worst case, the state would return to a dictatorship after the EU task force has left.

Such an approach would have immediately given the Iraqi people at least a local administration with a democratic legitimation in a large area of its territory. This would have been possible in the areas of the Kurds, the Shiites, and even in some larger Sunni areas. In reality, however, a different solution was applied. Military units with excellent training for fighting a war, but without any training as a police force, were expected to maintain law and order immediately after the fighting had ended in a state where the rule of law had been destroyed many years ago. In such a situation, the army of the liberator rapidly becomes the army of occupation. Without doubt, this made it much easier for the supporters of the old dictatorship in Iraq, together with other extremist forces, to organize armed resistance.

Besides the total collapse of law and order immediately after the liberation of Iraq, an additional reason for the rapid loss of sympathy and credibility was the inability of coalition forces to repair important parts of the destroyed infrastructure. In the planning stage, the EU task force in close cooperation with the United States could have made a comprehensive study of the condition of the infrastructure, expected war damage, and how the infrastructure might be improved. Often it is possible not only to repair war damage, but with little additional effort, to actually improve the infrastructure—transport and communication networks, the supply of water and electricity, and so on. It is important also to make early plans for the possibility of a refugee problem and how to care for and house refugees.

The extent to which local companies and local labor might be used should also have been investigated at the planning stage. The faster the local economy takes off, the smaller the danger that terrorist networks will emerge or that guerrilla warfare will break out. A high unemployment rate, especially if there are many unemployed people with military training as there were in Iraq, helps local and foreign extremists to delay or even prevent the establishment of an economically successful democratic state with the rule of law. For military intervention to succeed, the people must see rapid improvements compared to the situation in the old dictatorship. This is only possible if from the beginning the framework for the state is shaped as described in Chapters 10 and 11.

Before the general election for a parliament and the formation of a government, the EU task force would have to privatize state companies, even though such a move would be unpopular with large segments of the population. In this case, proceeds from the sale of state property should be used to finance the funded pension system as described in Chapter 10.2, and not to pay back the national debt. Whoever does business with and gives credit to an inhumane dictatorship has to know that certain risks are involved and that loans might not be repaid.

The rapid privatization of state enterprises, especially of the infrastructure, is important for another reason. In a dictatorship, but unfortunately not only there, state enterprises are all too often used to employ and serve the friends and supporters of the dictatorship. In addition, these are only rarely well-managed, modern enterprises, and retaining them would delay or even prevent economic development. If privatization is left until after the general election and the formation of the government, there is a danger that supporters of the old dictatorship in state enterprises will be fired, even if they are honest and competent, to be replaced by supporters of the new government who might be neither.

Only after local elections have been held, local administrations have started to work at their new tasks, and the newly trained local police forces and judges have taken up their responsibilities, does it make sense to hold parliamentary elections and appoint a new constitutional administration. Until then a provisional government would be in office that would have to cooperate closely with the representatives of the EU.

Even if the proposed model had been used in Iraq, it might have been difficult for EU police units to restore law and order within a reasonable time frame and at reasonable cost inside the so-called Sunni Triangle. Experience shows that with the support of part of the local population, it is rather easy to initiate acts of terrorism and guerrilla warfare in cities or in difficult terrain. In such a situation, the best strategy is probably to cut off and isolate the region and to prevent the spread of terrorist activities to other regions. Refugees should, of course, have the chance to leave the region, and strictly humanitarian aid should be let in. Highly mobile police units equipped with helicopters, surveillance drones, and other high-tech equipment should be able to cut off those areas with the support of American military units. Step by step, areas that are easier to control would be occupied, with the aim of isolating the different centers of terrorism and giving the refugees the possibility of returning. However, it would take time and patience for law and order to be restored in all regions and local elections to be held.

It would be wrong if development toward a democratic constitutional state were to be slowed down significantly or stopped only because it was taking so much longer in one region than others. If, for instance, it was not possible to restore law and order in one part of the Sunni Triangle within a certain time span, this area would have be separated from the rest of Iraq. In the more peaceful parts of the country, elections for parliament would take place and the government would be appointed; step by step, the state of the future would be realized with its responsibilities for foreign policy and the maintenance of law and order. Only when this process had come to a positive end should the EU task force withdraw its last police units and judges and give local communities the right of self-determination. In the state of the future, there would probably be no reason even for Kurdish communities in Iraq to leave the state, all the more because the Kurds have always been divided among themselves on both political and other lines. Many Kurds might be afraid to find themselves part of a nationalistic and socialistic Kurdish state and might prefer to remain citizens of the state of the future.

A politically and economically successful Iraq, integrated into the world economy and a member of the EEA, would become more and more attractive for those areas of the Sunni Triangle where it had not previously been possible to establish democracy and the rule of law. Support for the terrorists would decline because they would never be in a position to offer any future for a population that was completely dependent on external humanitarian aid.

There is much to be said for determining the maximum time frame for any intervention before it takes place. The fundamental problem is twofold. On the one hand, it takes years to build a modern, democratic, economically successful constitutional state, as described in Chapters 10 and 11. On the other hand, the proposed time frame should not be too long, as that would create a number of new problems, specifically:

1. A long-lasting intervention weakens reformist forces in the state and turns it into a de facto colony of the EU.

2. Without a clearly defined time frame, which is to be adhered to even in the case of failure, anti-democratic forces are strengthened. A number of member states of the EU were once colonial powers and could be quickly accused of colonialism, even if this was unjustified. The anti-democratic forces would then try to legitimize themselves through religion or an ideology such as nationalism.

3. A time limit obliges those political forces that are interested in maintaining the state to cooperate with the EU in the process of building a democratic constitutional state, because otherwise the state will fall apart as a result of the right of self-determination.

4. An intervention that remains unsuccessful after many years commits EU resources that could be better used elsewhere. Furthermore, political support in the member states for future missions will be undermined.

5. Even a failed intervention, which has been concluded within the predetermined time frame, offers the opportunity to analyze mistakes, to review the concept, and to implement improvements.

Provided that the United States and the EU were to provide sufficient human and material resources from the beginning, the first phase of any intervention could be concluded within four years. To return to the example of Iraq, 200,000 soldiers would have successfully completed the purely military aspect of the intervention. A further 200,000 people, supplied by the EU, would have ensured law and order and train police forces and judges. US troops could have been withdrawn from peaceful areas where local elections had been held and would have been transferred to those areas where, due to a lack of security, no local elections were held. Within these four years, the destroyed infrastructure would have been rebuilt or improved in order to privatize it alongside other state-owned enterprises by the end of the four-year period.

Upon successful completion of the first phase, the remaining US troops would have been withdrawn, and nationwide parliamentary elections held. In this second phase a democratically legitimized government would have set out to prove with the support of the EU that a state, as prescribed in Chapters 10 and 11, is beneficial for the entire population. Toward the end of this second phase, the population would be given the opportunity to exercise the right to self-determination at local level and thus to withdraw from the federal state. If this right was not exercised within a few months, the EU could begin to withdraw its police units and judges and gradually transfer the responsibility for law and order to the new, democratically legitimized government.

If certain local communities, cities, or regions vote to withdraw from the federal state during this second phase, the decision is to be respected. It is also possible that there will be municipalities and regions that reject the fundamental principles of the democratic constitutional state and the market economy. This wish would also have to be respected, but membership in the EEA would of course no longer be possible. Aid programs of the EU and other organizations and states would have to be stopped in such a case and limited resources concentrated on those regions that are prepared to commit to the fundamental principles of the democratic constitutional state and the market economy.

The second phase, like the first, would have to be concluded within four years. A successful intervention should result in one or more democratic states that are integrated economically into the EEA and are responsible for their own domestic security. The United States or the EU would be responsible for guaranteeing external security. This assurance would be of particular importance for a state like Iraq in case it falls apart into Kurdish, Shiite, and Sunni areas.

It would be a very positive development if the EU could somehow manage to realize an intervention of this kind during the next few years. The example of Bosnia-Herzegovina, admittedly on a smaller scale, closer geographically to the EU, and not yet a success, shows what can be achieved by a combination of the use of military and police task forces and the possibility of integration into the EU. The people in the "invaded" states would be happy, the United States would be happy, and the EU could show to the world an exemplary economic and political success.

Perhaps economic associations such as the North American Free Trade Agreement or the Association of Southeast Asian Nations might join in the economic reconstruction of those states by offering either direct or indirect membership in their associations. As the example of the Principality of Liechtenstein shows, membership of the EEA does not exclude membership of other economic associations in which industrial products and services are subject to different regulations.

Nevertheless, for a long time there will still be states in which there are serious violations of human rights, but where military intervention is not possible for various reasons. As with the former Soviet Union, the democratic constitutional states will have to content themselves with standing by and trying to prevent the further spread of such dictatorships which violate human rights.

There is always the hope that sooner or later leaders might emerge who are willing to make fundamental reforms, as in the Soviet Union. The model of the state of the future, as described here, gives political leaders greater possibilities for reforming the state rather than destroying it, as happened with the reforms of Gorbachev.

It might well be that this new state model is easier to realize in developing countries than in the highly developed states of the West. The transfer of the European and the American state model to the Third World has with few exceptions not been very successful. Third World countries have little to lose but much to gain by introducing a new state model.

It would not be the first time in history when less developed regions of the world have overtaken states in the more highly developed regions through fundamental reforms and a new state model. We have only to think about Persia, Ancient Greece, the Roman Empire, Europe of the second millennium, or the United States and Japan in the 19th and 20th centuries. In the globalized world of the third millennium, such developments will probably take place much faster and perhaps more peacefully than in the past, comparable to the competition between companies in a free globalized market economy.

13. A perspective on the third millennium

With the first human, a strange being stepped on to this planet—a being with a certain genetic relationship to the apes and other animals, but in some fundamental ways different from all the animals that have lived here over the last 500 million years. Genetically and behaviorally humans had to adapt very little to their environment, but nevertheless they spread very rapidly over all continents and climatic zones with the exception of Antarctica. In areas to which humans were not genetically suited, they understood rapidly how to adapt their immediate environment to their needs, for example by building houses and boats and making clothes to protect themselves against bad weather. Our different skin colors should not mislead us: under the skin human beings are hardly different from Australia to Greenland. The genetic difference between two neighboring groups of chimpanzees in the same African jungle seems to be greater than that between an Eskimo and an Australian Aboriginal.

All nationalistic ideologues as well as enemies of globalization should remember this when they divide humanity into different races and when they want to establish reservations to prevent the exchange of genes, goods, and services between them. Those enemies of globalization who jet across the planet from one demonstration to another particularly lack credibility. Many of them are certainly idealists with the best of intentions, but like the young idealists in the 20th century who were inspired by dangerous ideologies that ignored human rights, their actions might achieve the exact opposite of what they hope for. Instead of stressing the differences between human beings and thereby stirring up conflicts, we should emphasize what we have in common and search for solutions that make it possible for all people to live in peace, freedom, and prosperity.

Whether we like it or not, we human beings are a large family who often quarrel but equally can love each other. There will always be differences of opinion and quarrels, but they do not have to lead to murder and war. Buddhism, Christianity, and other important religions have long taught us that we should behave well even towards our enemies, as if they were our neighbors or family members. What important figures have recognized as right hundreds or even thousands of years ago is more true in our time of globalization and rapid technical progress. Murder and war might have shaped human history to a large extent, but less and less can we afford such behavior. On the one hand, modern transportation and communications have brought humanity much closer together; and on the other, modern technology has given smaller and smaller groups access to the most terrible weapons.

The wheel of history cannot be turned back. Humanity has to recognize as quickly as possible that the ideologies of the 19th and 20th centuries were dangerous cul-de-sacs. If humanity wants to survive in the long run, it has to break out of these dead ends of evolution. Perhaps for the first time, there is the possibility of turning states into peaceful service companies, which will not only serve oligarchs and monarchs, elected or not.

For this transformation process to succeed, it is not sufficient to create traditional states with the rule of law, indirect democracy, and a monopoly on their territory. This model has failed over the last two hundred years; and even where it does function more or less well, it seems as if the people work mainly for the state and not the other way around. The process of transforming the state from a demi-god into a service company that serves the people will only be possible if direct democracy replaces indirect democracy, and if the state's monopoly on its territory is broken up by the right of self-determination at local community level.

For many people this might look like utopia, especially for those people living in states that are still far from being democracies with the rule of law. However, have not many visions of past centuries become reality? Should humanity cling desperately to a state model that dates from the agrarian age? One thing is fairly certain: in the third millennium the state model of the agrarian age will sooner or later disappear, just as the state model of the hunter-gatherers has disappeared. The only question is whether it will disappear peacefully or in a world war with weapons of mass destruction.

If hunter-gatherers required a large territory to feed themselves, the necessary territory shrank drastically during the agrarian age. Before the agrarian age, nearly everyone had to look for food in order to survive, while now, at the end of the agrarian age, a farmer can feed ninety-nine people and the area required has become smaller and smaller because of higher yields. This development is far from over. This planet can feed many more people if our scientific knowledge is used in a sensible way and the environment is protected accordingly. Worldwide, the number of farmers will fall drastically in the future. In addition, modern agriculture has hardly anything in common with traditional agriculture.

The process of globalization advances rapidly, and those states that believe they can escape this process will not survive in the long term because they will simply not be sufficiently competitive. Globalization makes us into the large family that we have always been in reality. Today, humanity has to choose if it wants to shape this transformation process more or less peacefully or if it wants to proceed, as in the past, but with weapons that have become increasingly dangerous and that might one day destroy humanity and its environment.

The study of history reveals that states have life cycles just like the individual humans who created them. They come and they go, they are born, they grow, their frontiers change, they decay and dissolve again. This is a natural process, which people should contemplate in a more relaxed way and be prepared to shape peacefully.

Hardly any state existed inside its present borders two hundred years ago. States like France, Spain, Portugal, or England with their colonial empires were larger than today and others like the United States much smaller. The United States grew much larger only during the 19th century through the conquest of large areas in the south and west and the acquisition of Alaska. Even Switzerland increased its national territory in the middle of the 19th century. The Principality of Liechtenstein is one of the very few exceptions whose territory has not changed over the last two hundred years.

The coming and going, the growth and decay of states, have unfortunately rarely been peaceful processes: revolutions, civil wars, and wars of conquest accompanied both the birth of states and their disappearance. Homo erectus, two million years ago, was probably not a peaceful man, and one can assume that he decided disputes over his territory on the battlefield with his weapon in hand. I doubt whether we can afford this luxury in the third millennium. In deciding the life cycle of a state, the weapon in hand on the battlefield should be replaced with the ballot in hand at the ballot box according to the rule of law in a democratic state.

Physically, socially, and genetically humanity is still in the age of the hunter-gatherer, and intellectually and in state structures in the agrarian age; but in reality the age of space travel has already started. At the beginning of the space age, we can see that completely new dimensions are opening up for humanity. We have only to grasp them instead of fighting each other. At the end of the 20th century, individual states in national competition—with substantial financial expense and technical effort—opened up the door of the space age. At the beginning of the 21st century, private business is gradually taking over the role of the state in space. For most people it is still very difficult to imagine that the future of mankind lies in space. Yet it was also impossible for the first people in Africa to imagine that humans from Africa would settle over most of the planet in about 100,000 years.

Humanity will probably overcome the limits of our solar system and spread over the galaxy in a shorter time than was necessary to settle our planet. The often heard argument that no spaceship can fly faster than light, and that therefore humanity cannot overcome these huge distances within a reasonable time span, seems, after careful analysis of the theories of Einstein and others, to be perhaps not the insurmountable hurdle that is often maintained. To deal with this question in more detail would go beyond the scope of this book, but there are theories in physics indicating that these huge distances can possibly be overcome in a relatively short time. Eminent scientists have been meeting regularly and privately over a number of years to discuss such theories. The American space agency NASA has also organized such meetings to discuss possible technologies that might one day replace conventional rocket science and make space travel beyond our solar system possible.

In the 19th century the idea that people might one day fly to the moon was pure utopia. At that time scientists had no serious theories that would have made such flights possible. In the second half of the 20th century, man flew to the moon and landed there. At the beginning of the 21st century, there are theories about how to realize manned interstellar space flights with a short traveling time, but it will probably be decades before science can prove with certainty that those theories can be realized in practice. And it might be centuries before humanity starts to settle all over our galaxy. Nevertheless, surprises are always possible in science. Any 19th-century scientist who dared to predict that less than a century later people would fly to the moon would have been called an unrealistic dreamer. A scientist who dares now, at the beginning of the third millennium, to predict that humanity will be technically able to settle the galaxy at the end of the third millennium could turn out to be overcautious.

Research during the last few years has shown that life on planet earth has been almost destroyed several times over the last 800 million years due to extreme climate changes. We do not know exactly why those climatic disasters occurred, but calculations show that a collision with a celestial body, whose diameter is only a few kilometers, could lead to such catastrophic effects. There are thousands of such celestial bodies in our solar system, whose orbits vary considerably and therefore cannot be calculated exactly over long periods of time. We humans are all sitting here on planet earth in the same boat. Instead of waging wars with each other, we should, first of all, ensure that this boat is in excellent condition so that future generations can live on it and, second, make an effort to guarantee that one day humanity has additional boats at its disposal.

To settle our galaxy would be a very large step for humanity. Nevertheless, it is a step that from today's viewpoint is smaller than the settlement of the polar regions by a being originating in the hot regions of Africa. The human mind was able to overcome all those obstacles. It is not the large distances that are the obstacle but our intellect, which is still strongly shaped by the behavior and thinking patterns of the agrarian age. We have to free ourselves from these bonds to give humanity the freedom to open up new dimensions.

Appendix: A draft constitution for the state in the third millennium

Constitution of the kingdom X [the republic Y]

Chapter I: The kingdom X [the republic Y]

Article 1

1) The kingdom X [the republic Y] is a state confederation on a democratic and parliamentary basis which shall serve the people within its borders so that they can live together in freedom, peace, and prosperity.

2) The authority of the state is vested in and issues from the king [president] and the people. It shall be exercised by both in accordance with the provisions of this constitution.

Article 2

1) It is the duty of the state to represent the interests of the people and the state in relations with other states, state confederations, and similar organizations.

2) It is the duty of the state to issue laws and decrees which enable the people to live in freedom, peace, and prosperity, especially those regulations concerning education, social security, health, transportation, and the environment and regulations concerning the autonomy and the duties of the local communities.

3) It is the duty of the state to ensure that the constitution, the laws, and the decrees are observed. To serve this purpose the state will finance the courts, the state prosecution authorities, and the police.

4) It is not the duty of the state to own or to administer institutions, which are active in education, social security, health, transportation, or any other area. These institutions are to be owned and administered by local communities, associations of local communities, private business, or private organizations.

Article 3

1) To finance its activities, the state is entitled to all the revenues from indirect taxation such as value added tax, customs duties, or other duties where applicable. The local communities are entitled to tax sovereignty in respect of all direct taxation on individuals and legal entities, whereby the state has the authority to lay down the basic rules concerning direct taxation to avoid abuses and conflicts between the local communities.

2) The state shall be sparing with its revenues and shall achieve each year surpluses which are to be distributed to the local communities in proportion to the number of their inhabitants. A portion of the surpluses may be distributed by the state according to the law in the form of educational vouchers to persons who are subject to compulsory school attendance.

3) The state is not permitted to issue guarantees or to raise loans except in special situations, which are to be covered by law. Those laws are subject to referendum in accordance with Article 31. After ten years at the latest loans have to be repaid through surpluses of the state and guarantees cancelled.

Article 4

1) Changes in the boundaries of the territory of the kingdom [republic] may be made only by virtue of law. The individual local communities have the right to leave the state confederation. The majority of the citizens with voting rights residing in the community shall decide about the initiation of the proceedings for a withdrawal of the community from the state. The procedure for withdrawal can be regulated either through law or by a state treaty on a case-by-case basis. In the case of a state treaty a second vote shall take place in the local community after the treaty negotiations have been concluded.

2) Changes of boundaries between local communities, the creation of new local communities, and the merger of existing ones require a majority vote by the citizens with voting rights who reside in those local communities.

APPENDIX: A DRAFT CONSTITUTION FOR THE STATE IN THE THIRD MILLENNIUM

Chapter II: The king [The president]

Article 5

The succession to the throne, hereditary in the Royal House, the coming of age of the king and of the crown prince, as well as any guardianship which may be required, are to be determined by the laws of the Royal House.

[The president shall be elected in a free and secret vote by the citizens with voting rights for a period of office of four years. Re-election is possible. The election of the president has to take place six weeks before the four-year period in office comes to an end or six weeks after the presidency has become prematurely vacant. If the presidency has become prematurely vacant due to the death or resignation of the president or through removal from office (Article 12), the president of the parliament shall take over the duties of the state president until a new president is elected.

Should more than two candidates apply for the presidency, each citizen with voting rights shall have two votes in the first round of the election. He shall cast those two votes for the two candidates whom he wishes to take part in the second round of the election. Those two candidates who have received the most first and second votes shall take part in the second election. In the second election, which has to take place fourteen days after the first election, each citizen with voting rights shall have one vote. The candidate who has received the absolute majority of the votes is elected.]

Article 6

1) The king [president] is the head of state and shall exercise his sovereign authority in conformity with the provisions of this constitution and of the other laws.

2) The king [president] as a person is not subject to the judicial proceedings and is legally not responsible. The same applies to the member of the Royal House [president of the parliament], who exercises in accordance with Article 11 the functions of head of state for the king [president].

Article 7

1) The king [president] shall represent the state in all its relations with foreign countries without prejudice to the necessary participation of the responsible government.

2) Treaties by which national territories are ceded, national property is disposed of, rights of sovereignty or state prerogatives are disposed of, any new burden for the kingdom [republic] or its citizens is imposed, or any obligation to the detriment of the rights of the citizens is contracted shall not be valid, unless they have received the assent of the parliament.

Article 8

1) Every law, the budget, loans, taxes, and other state duties (Article 3) shall require the sanction of the king [president] in order to be valid.

2) In urgent cases the king [president] shall take the necessary measures by emergency decree for the security and welfare of the state. Emergency decrees cannot abolish the constitution as a whole or individual articles of the constitution, but can only restrict the application of certain articles of the constitution. Emergency decrees cannot restrict either the right of each person to live, the prohibition of torture and inhuman treatment, the prohibition of slavery and forced labor, or the rule of no punishment without law. In addition, the provisions of this Article, of Articles 5, 12, and 47 as well as the law of the Royal House, cannot be restricted by emergency decrees. Emergency decrees shall cease to be in force at the latest six months after they have been issued.

3) The king [president] shall appoint judges in accordance with the provisions of this constitution (Article 39).

Article 9

1) The king [president] shall possess the prerogative of remitting, mitigating, or commuting sentences which have been legally pronounced and of terminating prosecutions which have been initiated.

2) Only at the instigation of parliament shall the king [president] exercise his prerogative of remission or mitigation in favor of a member of the government sentenced on account of his official acts.

Article 10

Every successor to the throne [president] shall before receiving the oath of allegiance [before taking office] declare in a written document that he will govern the kingdom [republic] according to the constitution and the other laws.

Article 11

The king may entrust the next heir apparent of his house who has attained majority with the exercise of the sovereign powers held by him as his representative should he be temporarily unable to perform his functions or in preparation for the succession.

[The president may entrust the president of the parliament with the exercise of the sovereign powers held by him as his representative should he be temporarily unable to perform his functions.]

Article 12

At least 5 percent of the citizens with voting rights may introduce, with the reason stated, a vote of no confidence in the king. The parliament must give a recommendation on this vote of no confidence at its next meeting and must put the vote of no confidence to a popular vote (Article 30). If the motion of no confidence is accepted by the popular vote the king has to be notified, so that the case can be dealt with in accordance with the law of the Royal House. Within six months the king shall inform the parliament of the decision taken in accordance with the law of the Royal House.

[At least 5 percent of the citizens with voting rights may introduce, with the reason stated, a vote of no confidence in the president. The parliament must give a recommendation on this vote of no confidence at its next meeting and must put the vote of no confidence to a popular vote (Article 30). If the motion of no confidence is accepted by the popular vote, the constitutional court (Article 43 shall decide within six months whether the president is to be removed from office.]

Chapter III: General rights and obligations of citizens

Article 13

1) All citizens shall be equal before the law. The public offices shall be equally open to them, subject to observance of the legal regulations.

2) There shall be equality of rights between the sexes.

3) The law regulates the acquisition and loss of citizenship.

4) The rights of aliens shall be determined in the first instance by treaties or in the absence of such on the basis of reciprocity.

Article 14

1) Every citizen shall be freely entitled to reside in any locality within the territory of the state and to acquire property of any description, provided that he observes the detailed legal regulations relating to such matters.

2) Persons residing within the territory of the state shall be bound to observe its laws and shall be entitled to the protection afforded by the constitution and the other laws.

Article 15

1) All citizens shall be entitled to civic rights in conformity with the provisions of this constitution.

2) All citizens who have completed their eighteenth year, who have their normal residence in the state, and whose right to vote has not been revoked, may exercise all political rights in matters of the state and his local community.

Article 16

1) Personal liberty, the immunity of the home, and the inviolability of the post are guaranteed.

2) Except in the cases specified in law and in the manner thus prescribed, no person may be arrested or detained in custody, no houses, letters or written matter, or persons may be searched, and no letters or written matter may be seized.

Appendix: A draft constitution for the state in the third millennium

3) Persons arrested unlawfully or demonstrably innocent and those proved innocent after conviction shall be entitled to full compensation from the state as determined by the courts. Whether and to what extent the state has a right of recourse against third parties in such cases shall be regulated by law.

Article 17

1) Nobody may be deprived of his proper judge; special tribunals may not be instituted.

2) Nobody may be threatened with or subjected to penalties other than those provided by the law.

3) Accused persons shall have the right of defense in all penal proceedings.

Article 18

1) The inviolability of private property is guaranteed.

2) Where necessary in the public interest, property of any kind may be compulsorily assigned or subjected to an encumbrance, against appropriate compensation, the amount of which in cases of dispute shall be determined by the courts.

3) The procedure for expropriation shall be regulated by law.

Article 19

Trade and industry shall be free within the limits prescribed by law; the extent to which exclusive commercial and industrial privileges may be admissible for specified periods of time shall be regulated by law.

Article 20

The freedom of belief and conscience is guaranteed for all persons. All religions are entitled to practice their creeds and to hold religious services to the extent consistent with morality and public order.

Article 21

1) Every person shall be entitled freely to express his opinion and to communicate his ideas by word of mouth or in writing, print or pictures within the limits of the law and morality.

2) The right of free association and assembly is guaranteed within the limits prescribed by law.

Chapter IV: The parliament

Article 22

The parliament represents the people in all those cases in which in accordance with the constitution the people do not decide themselves. The parliament has the following rights:

a) to participate in the work of legislation and in the conclusion of treaties;

b) to propose to the king [president] the members of the government and to withdraw its confidence from them;

c) to participate in the appointment of judges;

d) to approve the state budget and loans (Article 3), as well as taxes and duties (Article 3);

e) to control over the whole state administration. The parliament's right of control does not extend either to the judgments of the courts or to the activities allocated to the king [president].

Article 23

1) The parliament consists of twenty-five representatives, who shall be elected by the people by universal, equal, secret, and direct suffrage. The mandates shall be distributed among electoral groups, which have obtained at least 4 percent of the valid votes cast in the state as a whole.

2) Each electoral group has the right to nominate for each of its representatives one substitute who shall deputize for the representative in case he cannot take part in a meeting of the parliament. The representative who cannot participate must inform the president of the parliament in due time.

3) Members of the government and the courts cannot be simultaneously members of parliament.

4) Detailed regulations regarding the conduct of the election shall be laid down in a special law.

Article 24

Within four weeks after the election of the parliament the king [president] shall convene and open the parliament's constituent assembly. At this constituent assembly the parliament shall elect its president and his deputy. Further meetings of the parliament shall be convened by the president of the parliament or his deputy. Apart from the king [president], the president of the parliament, and his deputy, the representatives have the right to convene parliament should at least eight of them require it.

Article 25

The representatives shall be elected for four years. The king [president] or the people respectively have the right to dissolve the parliament and to order new elections. These have to take place within two months after the parliament has been dissolved. Five percent of the citizens with voting rights have the right to put forward a proposal for a popular vote to dissolve the parliament.

Article 26

1) No representative may be arrested while the parliament is in session without the assent of that body unless he is apprehended in flagrante delicto.

2) In the latter case, the arrest and the grounds therefor must be notified forthwith to the parliament, which shall decide whether the arrest is to be sustained. All documentation relating to the case must be placed immediately at the disposal of the parliament, if it so requests.

3) If a representative is arrested at a time when the parliament is not in session, the president of the parliament must be notified forthwith and informed at the same time of the grounds for the arrest.

Article 27

1) All members of parliament shall swear the following oath to the king [president] at the opening of the parliament (Article 24):

"I hereby swear to observe the state constitution and the existing laws and to promote in the parliament the welfare of the state without any ulterior motives to the best of my ability and conscience."

2) The members of parliament shall vote solely in accordance with their oath and their convictions. They shall never be made to answer for their votes;

for their utterances at sittings of the parliament or its committees, they shall be responsible to the parliament alone and can never be arraigned before a court of justice in respect thereof. The exercise of disciplinary powers shall be regulated by rules of procedure to be issued hereafter.

3) The parliament shall adopt its rules of procedure by resolution and with due regard to the provisions of this constitution. These rules shall regulate, among other matters, the formation of the different commissions of the parliament, the elections and votes in the parliament, and the remuneration of the representatives.

Article 28

The parliament shall scrutinize the validity of the election of its members and of the election as such on the basis of the election records and, if applicable, of the decisions of the constitutional court. Complains relating to elections shall be referred to the constitutional court.

Article 29

1) The right of initiative with regard to legislation belongs to:

a) the king [president];

b) the parliament;

c) the government;

d) the citizens with voting rights when at least 5 percent of them present such an initiative.

2) If the initiative involves public expenditure, whether in a single sum or in payments extending over a longer period, such an initiative shall only be discussed by the parliament if it is accompanied by proposals for providing the necessary funds.

3) Initiatives which are in accordance with this constitution shall be debated, if possible, at the next session of the parliament, but at the latest after six weeks.

Article 30

1) Laws, treaties (Article 7), loans, taxes, and duties (Article 3) passed by parliament shall be submitted to a popular vote if the parliament so decides,

or if not less than 5 percent of the citizens with voting rights submit a proposal to that effect within six weeks of the official publication of the resolution of the parliament.

2) Resolutions of the parliament subject to a referendum shall be submitted to the king [president] for sanction after the referendum has been held or after the statutory period of six weeks within which a petition for a referendum may be submitted has expired without any such action.

3) If the parliament rejects a law which has been submitted to it through the procedure of the popular initiative (Article 29.1d) the said law shall be submitted to a referendum within six weeks. The parliament has the right to submit to the people a counter-proposal. The popular vote replaces the otherwise necessary resolution by the parliament. The acceptance or rejection of the resolution on the enactment of the law shall be decided by an absolute majority of the valid votes recorded in the whole state.

4) Further detailed regulations regarding the initiative and the referendum shall be issued in the form of a law.

Article 31

1) With regard to the state administration, the government shall submit to the parliament for examination and approval preliminary estimates of all expenditure and revenues for the coming administrative year, accompanied by proposals for the taxation which is to be levied.

2) In the first half of each administrative year the government shall submit to the parliament an exact statement relating to the preceding year showing the manner in which revenues approved and collected were applied for the purposes set out in the preliminary estimates, with the provision, however, that if the latter have been exceeded on justifiable grounds the parliament must give its approval and that in the absence of justification the government shall be answerable.

3) The government shall be entitled to incur expenditure of an urgent character not provided for in the preliminary estimates, subject to the same conditions as above.

4) Economies effected in the case of individual items of the preliminary estimates may not be used to cover excess expenditure on other items.

Article 32

1) Unless it contains any other stipulation, a law shall come into force on the expiry of eight days after the date of its publication in the national legal gazette.

2) The manner and extent of the publication of laws, finance resolutions, treaties, regulations, and resolutions of international organizations and of measures deriving from international treaties shall be regulated by law. For measures applicable in the kingdom [republic] by reason of international treaties, publication may be arranged in a simplified form, in particular as a reference publication to foreign law.

Chapter V: The government

Article 33
1) Subject to the provisions of this article, the whole of the state administration shall be conducted by the government responsible to the king [president] and the parliament in conformity with the provisions of this constitution and the other laws.

2) Specific functions may be transferred by law or by legally binding authorizations to individual officials, government offices, or special commissions for independent execution, subject to recourse to the government.

Article 34
1) The government shall consist of the prime minister and four ministers.

2) The prime minister and the ministers shall be appointed by the king [president] with the concurrence of the parliament and on the proposal of the latter. A substitute shall be appointed in like manner for the prime minister and for each minister to represent the member of government in question should he be unable to attend the meetings of the government.

3) The prime minister and the other members of the government shall swear the following oath to the king [president]:

"I hereby swear to observe the state constitution and the existing laws and to promote the welfare of the state without any ulterior motives to the best of my ability and conscience."

4) The period of office of the government shall be four years, subject to the provisions of Article 37.

Article 35
1) The government is responsible for executing all the laws and for carrying out all the orders of the king [president] or of the parliament which are permitted by law.

2) The government shall issue the decrees needed to implement the laws and treaties which are directly applicable, which can only be issued within the framework of the law and the treaties which are directly applicable.

3) To realize other treaty obligations, the government can issue the necessary decrees as far as there is no need to issue a law.

4) The whole state administration must act entirely within the framework of the constitution, the laws and the applicable treaties; in those matters where the law gives the administration the freedom to act on its own discretion, the framework stipulated by the law must also be strictly observed.

Article 36

The following matters in particular shall fall within the domain of the government:

a) the supervision of the state administration;

b) the appointment and dismissal of public servants with the exception of judges or public servants of the parliament;

c) the drawing up of the yearly budget and of the report on its activities for the past year, to be submitted annually to the king [president] and parliament;

d) the drawing up of its rules of procedure, which are to be published.

Article 37

1) If the government loses the confidence of the king [president] or of the parliament, their authority to carry out government duties expires. Until a new government assumes office, the king [president] shall appoint a caretaker government to take care of the whole state administration. The king [president] can also appoint members of the old government to the caretaker government. Within four months the caretaker government must receive a vote of confidence in the parliament insofar as the king [president] has not appointed a new government with the concurrence of the parliament and on the proposal of the latter (Article 34).

2) If an individual member of the government loses the confidence of the king [president] or the parliament, the decision about his deprival of office will be taken in concurrence between the king [president] and the parliament. Until the appointment of a new member of government his deputy must take carry out his government duties.

Chapter VI: The courts

A. General provisions

Article 38

1) The whole administration of justice shall be carried out in the name of the king [president] and the people by judges who are appointed by the king [president] (Article 8). Decisions and judgments by the judges are to be issued in the name of the king [president] and the people.

2) The judges shall be independent when exercising their judicial office, within the limits of the law and when engaged in judicial proceedings. Their decisions and judgments shall be accompanied by a statement of reasons. Only where the constitution expressly foresees it (Article 9) may the administration of justice be influenced by another state institution.

3) Judges within the meaning of this article are the judges of all the normal courts (Articles 40 und 41), the judges of the administrative court (Article 42) as well as the judges of the constitutional court (Article 43).

Article 39

1) For the selection of the judges the king [president] and the parliament shall institute a joint committee. The king [president] shall preside and in the event of a tied vote shall have the casting vote. He can nominate as many members for this committee as the parliament. The parliament delegates one representative for each electoral group represented in the parliament. The government delegates the minister of justice. The deliberations of the committee are confidential. The committee can only recommend candidates to the parliament with the consent of the king [president]. If the parliament elects the recommended candidate he shall then be appointed as judge by the king [president].

2) Should the parliament reject the candidate recommended by the committee and if there is no agreement on a new candidate within four weeks, then the parliament has to present an opposing candidate and order a popular vote. In the case of a popular vote the citizens with voting rights can also nominate a candidate according to the procedures for an initiative (Article 29). Should there be more than two candidates, the popular vote will take place in two elections in accordance with Article 47. The candidate who has received the absolute majority of the votes shall be appointed as judge by the king [president].

3) A judge appointed for a set term remains in office until his successor is sworn in. Further detailed provisions concerning the procedure, the right of abstention, emoluments, and the fees to be paid by the parties involved shall be stipulated in a special law.

B. The ordinary courts

Article 40

1) Jurisdiction shall be exercised in the first instance by the district court, in the second instance by the high court of appeal, and in the third instance by the supreme court.

2) By law certain types of cases of the first instance can be delegated to civil servants of the district court who are specially trained and subject to directives.

Article 41

The supreme court has disciplinary powers over the members of the normal courts and the civil servants of the courts.

C. The administrative court

Article 42

1) The administrative court consists of five judges and five substitute judges, who are appointed by the king [president] (Article 39). The majority of the judges must be citizens of the country.

2) The term of office of the judges and the substitute judges of the administrative court is five years. The term of office is to be structured in a way that every year the term of one judge and one substitute judge comes to an end. At the first appointment the term of office of the five judges and the five substitute judges is decided by lot. Should a judge or a substitute judge retire prematurely from office, his successor is to be appointed for the remaining term of office of the retiring judge. Re-election is possible.

3) The five judges elect every year one of their members as a chairman and another as a deputy chairman.

4) If a judge is unable to attend a meeting, a substitute judge will represent him in this case. From case to case substitution has to take place by rotation.

5) Insofar as the law does not otherwise provide, all decisions and decrees of the government and of the commissions set up by the government (Article 33) can be appealed at the administrative court.

D. The constitutional court

Article 43

1) The constitutional court serves to protect the rights accorded by the constitution and to decide in conflicts of competence between the courts and the state administration.

2) The constitutional court also has the competence to determine whether laws and international treaties are in conformity with the constitution and whether the decrees of the government are in conformity with the laws; in cases where they are not in conformity it may declare their annulment. It shall also act as an electoral tribunal.

3) Otherwise the regulations of Article 42 apply accordingly.

Chapter VII: On the local communities and the administration

Article 44

Provisions concerning the organization and duties of the local communities in their own sphere of action and in tasks assigned to them shall be laid down by law.

In the law concerning the local communities the following principles shall be established:

a) the free election of the mayor and the council of the community by the citizens of the community;

b) the right of the community to grant citizenship and the freedom of citizens to reside in any community;

c) the right of the community to raise taxes (Article 3) and to administer the assets of the community;

d) the administration of the local police under the supervision of the government.

Article 45

1) The state, the local communities, and other corporations, establishments, and foundations of public law are liable for damage caused to third persons by individuals acting as their agents who act illegally in their official capacity.

2) Individuals acting as agents are answerable to the state, to the local community, to the establishment, to the foundation, or to other corporations of public law which they serve for any damage directly caused to such bodies through the willful or grossly negligent breach of their official duties.

3) Further detailed provisions, especially those relating to competence, shall be laid down in a separate law.

APPENDIX: A DRAFT CONSTITUTION FOR THE STATE IN THE THIRD MILLENNIUM

Chapter VIII: The maintenance of the constitution

Article 46

Amendments or generally binding interpretations of the constitution can be proposed either by the king [president], the parliament, or the government, or can be made through the procedure of an initiative (Article 29). They require on the part of the parliament approval either by unanimous vote of the representatives present or by a majority of three-quarters of the representatives present at two successive sittings of the parliament and, if required, a popular vote (Article 30). In each case the approval of the king [president] is necessary, with the exception of the procedures for the abolition of the monarchy [republic] (Article 47).

Article 47

1) At least 5 percent of the citizens with voting rights can introduce an initiative to abolish the monarchy [republic]. Should the initiative be accepted in a popular vote, the parliament has to formulate a new constitution for a republic [monarchy] and to order at the earliest after one year and at the latest after two years a popular vote. The king [president] has the right to propose a new constitution for the same popular vote. The procedure for changing the constitution in Article 46 is replaced in this case by the following procedure.

2) If there is only one proposal, an absolute majority is sufficient for acceptance (Article 30). If there are two proposals, each citizen with voting rights has the option of choosing between the existing constitution and the two proposals. In this case the citizen with voting rights shall have two votes in the first round of voting. He shall give those two votes to the two variants of the constitution which he wishes to put to the second vote. Those two variants of the constitution which have received the most first and second votes shall be the subjects of the second round of voting. In the second vote, which must take place fourteen days after the first vote, each citizen with voting rights shall have one vote. The constitution which has received the absolute majority of the votes is accepted (Article 30).

Chapter IX: Final provisions

Article 48

All laws, decrees, and statutory provisions which contradict any expressed provision of this constitution are hereby revoked and declared invalid; legal provisions which are inconsistent with the spirit of this fundamental law shall be revised to conform with the constitution.

Vaduz, December 11, 2007

Index

The abbreviation, tms, used in the sub-entries stands for: third millennium state.

A

agrarian age
  see also agrarian revolution
  advantages of, 50
  definition of borders in, 17
  property rights during, 92
  transition to, 24, 30, 32, 86
agrarian revolution
  see also agrarian age
  influence on development of states, 48–50, 107
  influence on state form, 54
  political consequences of, 51, 54, 85
agriculture
  changes in modern, 179
  influence of market economy on, 123–124
  loss of landscape molded by, 123–124
  state intervention in, 122
  in the tms model, 123–124
aid programs, 173
air supremacy, 40
Alexander the Great, 33, 51
Algeria, 5
American Constitution, 60, 61, 62, 77
American Revolution, 30, 55, 59, 62
anarchy
  after fall of part of the Roman Empire, 55
  definition of, 2, 19
  part in state cycle, 19, 45, 47
Anglican Church, 28
animal behavior, 21, 47
anti-aircraft missiles, 39

Arab world, 34, 148
arms race, 35, 41
artillery, 35, 41
Association of Southeast Asian Nations, 148–149, 174
Austria
  see also Habsburg Empire
  and economic ties with Liechtenstein, 11, 69
  lack of labor force in, 14
  legal developments in, 69, 101
  occupation by the Third Reich, 11
  ties with House of Liechtenstein, 6
Austro-Hungarian Empire, 137, 139
  see also Habsburg Empire
automobile industry, 113–114

B

Babenberg family, 6
bacteriological weapons, 86
banking, 138–141, 142–145
bankruptcies, 129–130
Basques (ethnic group), 5
Baudouin I, King of the Belgians, 56
"bazooka," 39
Bern (canton), 7
Bhagwati, Jagdish, 114
birth rate, 22, 23, 110
Bismarck, Otto von, 109
Bosnia-Herzegovina, 174
brain research, 22
Buddhism, 22
Burma (now Myanmar), 149

- 203 -

"buying votes," 83, 95–96, 128, 131
Byzantine Empire, 26, 27

C

Calvin, John, 65
Cambodia, 2–3
Canada, 9, 11
Carthage, 51–52
Catholic Church
   see Roman Catholic Church
cattle breeding, 24, 50, 53, 54
cavalry, 33, 37–38, 41, 53
Central Asia, 33, 44
centralization, political, 61
Charlemagne, 55
Charles I, Emperor of Austria, 7
Charles I, of the Holy Roman Empire, 55
Charles the Great, 55
chemical weapons, 86
China
   effects of globalization on, 114
   industrialization of, 36
   in the Korean War, 39–40
   political murders in, 2–3
   state model of ancient, 50
   and US military supremacy, 41
Chinese Empire, 136
Christianity
   see also Reformation
   legitimizing states through, 24–27
   and liberalism, 80
   negative attitude towards wealth, 27–28
   spread of, 25–26
churches, 27–28
Cicero, 19
cities, fortified, 32, 34, 49
citizens
   adaptation to tms model, 157–159
   and the knowledge of laws, 91, 94, 97–98
   rights and obligations in tms constitution, 152, 188–189
   states' interaction with, 81–82
city-states, 10, 32, 35
civil servants
   and behavior towards citizens, 100
   dismissal of, 96, 105–106
   independence of, 106
Civil War (USA), 62
civil war (Yugoslavia), 9
civil wars
   danger from, 148
   prevention of, 9, 52, 86–87
   in Roman Republic, 50
coinage, 135–136, 137–141
Cold War, 41, 42, 43, 148
colonial empires
   advantages of, 35–36
   artificial state creation by, 6
   collapse of, 14
   economic competitiveness, 13, 14
   seafaring states as, 12
communications network, 86, 147
communism
   and the collapse of Soviet Empire, 7–8
   difference between National Socialism and, 2–3
   ideology of sharing and equal distribution, 108
   isolation of private and public networks, 149
   and repression of religion, 23
   and the totalitarian state, 1
Communist Party (Soviet Union), 8
competition
   between currencies, 137, 141
   between tax policies, 130–131
   worldwide development of, 13, 14
Congress (USA), 67
Constantine I, Emperor, 26
constitutions
   see also American Constitution; Liechtenstein's constitution; Swiss constitution; third millennium state constitution
   adaptation after military intervention, 166
   changing power of monarchy through, 56
   content of, 93–94
   the preamble to, 151–152
   procedures for changing, 153–154, 201
   self-limiting of the state in, 95–97
Council of Europe, 103

The Council of Europe: Monitoring Procedures and the Constitutional Autonomy of the Member States, 103
courts of law, 153, 197–199
craftsmen, 54–55
crime, 91, 98–100
Croatia, 9
crop failure, 55
Cuius regio eius religio, 28
cultural institutions, 147
currencies
   adopting foreign, 137
   and competition between, 137, 141
   and exchange rates, 138
   and guaranteed metal, 138–141
   history of, 135–136
   influence on financial services industry, 142
   return to metal, 137–138
customs duties, 79
Czechoslovakia, 71

D

Danspeckgruber, Wolfgang, 14–15, 161
decentralization, political, 7, 160
decolonization, 6, 163
deep-sea fishing, 92–93
defense policy, 40–41, 148, 153
democracies
   see also democratic constitutional states; direct democracies; indirect democracies
   definition of, 18–19
   development of, 66, 77–78
   establishing after military intervention, 162–172
   and interaction with citizens, 81–82
   legitimizing states through, 19
   necessity of oligarchy in, 81–82
   part in state cycle, 19, 45, 47
   reasons for, 45
   and self-determination, 74–75
   in Stone Age tribal communities, 47
   and suffrage, 62, 63
democratic constitutional states
   see also democracies; direct democracies; indirect democracies

   adaptation to tms model, 157–161
   development towards, 171
   erosion of, 104
   independent justice system in, 101
   judges in, 102–103
   law enforcement in, 91
   laws and regulations of, 93–96
   and military interventions, 162–163
   minorities in, 87
democratic rights
   in direct democracies, 65–67
   erosions of, 54
   in indirect democracies, 61–62, 67–68
developing countries
   and the drugs trade, 99, 100
   education and, 168
   farming in, 123
   and foreign aid, 109, 149–150, 173
   and the tms model, 174–175
dictatorship, 161–162, 164–165, 166, 170
direct democracies
   see also indirect democracies
   integrating people into, 97
   Liechtenstein model of, 69, 70–73, 97, 119, 160–161
   shift toward, 160
   Swiss model of, 63, 65–68, 70, 97, 160–161
   voters in, 98
   weak forms of, 56
domestic markets, 13, 36
draft constitution
   see EU draft constitution; third millennium state constitution
drug addicts, 98, 99
drug problem, 98–100

E

Eastern Orthodox Church, 26, 29
economic crimes, 98
economic crisis 1929 of, 162
   see also financial crisis of 2008
economies
   see also storage economies; "the bigger the better" economic theory
   globalization of, 14, 78–81, 113–115

influence of Catholicism on, 27–28, 29
influence of Islam on, 34
Edict of Milan (313), 25
education
   and developing countries, 168
   and direct democracy, 62
   and teaching law in school, 94
   use of voucher system for, 117–119, 130, 150, 184
EEA (European Economic Area), 167, 172, 173, 174
EEC (European Economic Community), 42
Egypt, 32, 49–50
Egyptians, 17
emigration, 87, 88, 96, 113
emperors
   divine origins of, 24, 25, 26, 49, 51
   divine status of, 50, 53
The Enlightenment, 28
environment, 93, 122–123, 132, 159, 179
equality, 61, 188
equestrian armies, 33, 34, 44, 53–54
equity, 88, 143–144
ethnic cleansing, 9–10, 87
ethnic diversity, 8
ethnic minorities, 7, 9
ethnicity, 74–75
EU draft constitution, 154–155
EU (European Union)
   and the Council of Europe, 103
   and establishing democracy after military intervention, 165–174
   importance in foreign relations, 127, 148–149
   and increase in regulations, 94
   and Yugoslavia, 9
EU subsidies, 154
EU task force, 165–166, 167–171
euro, 137, 139–140, 165
Europe, 10, 11
   see also Western Europe
European Court of Justice, 103
European Defense Community, 42
European Economic Area (EEA), 167, 172, 173, 174

European Economic Community (EEC), 42
European Union (EU)
   see EU (European Union)
evolution
   see human evolution
exchange rates, 138

F
farmers, 54, 99, 123–124
farming, 48, 54, 179
fertile crescent, 32, 49
financial crisis of 2008, 142, 144, 145
   see also economic crisis of 1929
financial services industry, 142–145
   see also insurance industry
First World War, 37–38
fishing, 92–93
foreign aid, 109, 149, 173
foreign policy, 96–97, 147–149
fortified cities, 32, 34, 49
Founding Fathers (USA), 59–60, 61
France
   see also French monarchy; French Revolution; Napoleonic Empire
   and the arms race in artillery, 35
   canal system in, 12
   during Cold War, 43
   and the Suez crisis, 164
   unification of, 64
   and US military supremacy, 41–42
   in the Vietnam wars, 40
Franco-German War (1870), 37
Franco-Prussian War (1870), 37
Franz Ferdinand, Archduke of Austria, 7
Franz Josef II, Prince of Liechtenstein, 7, 72
Franz Joseph I, Emperor of Austria, 7
free trade, 79–80, 103
French monarchy, 29, 30, 63–64
French Revolution, 29, 30, 55, 63–64

G
gender equality, 188
geography, 31
German Confederation, 69
German Democratic Republic, 161

German Empire, 38, 109
Germany, 41–42, 162
  see also The Third Reich; German Empire; Holy Roman Empire (of German Nations)
globalization
  enemies of, 177
  and foreign policy, 148–149
  and influence on agriculture, 123–124
  and influence on nationalism and socialism, 78–80
  and influence on poverty in India and China, 114
  and influence on society, 86
  and international crime, 91, 98
  and paper currency, 136
  rapid advancement of, 179
  and reform of the financial services sector, 144
  and the welfare state, 109
  of world economy, 14, 78–81, 113–115
Gorbachev, Mikhail, 8, 174
government Spain (Franco), 5
government Switzerland, 7
governments
  see also civil servants
  different models of, 104–105
  duties and responsibilities in the tms constitution of, 153, 195–196
  legitimation of, 5–6
  size of, 104
Great Britain
  building colonial empires, 35
  colonies in North America, 59
  easy access by sea, 12
  as an oligarchy with democratic legitimation, 55–56
  state structure of, 60–61
  and the Suez crisis, 164
  and US military supremacy, 41–42
Greece
  see also Alexander the Great
  ancient city-states of, 10, 32, 49
  central role of religion in state authority of, 21
  easy access by sea, 12

guerrilla warfare, 100, 148, 171
guest workers, 11, 14
Gulf War, 148

H
Habsburg Empire
  see also Austro-Hungarian Empire
  and the arms race in artillery, 35
  collapse of, 7, 69
  customs agreement with Liechtenstein, 11
  ties with the House of Liechtenstein, 6–7, 69
  use of cavalry of, 33
  and WW I, 38
Habsburg monarchy
  see Habsburg Empire
Hannibal, 52
Hans-Adam II, Prince of Liechtenstein
  see also Princely House of Liechtenstein; third millennium state constitution
  address to Woodrow Wilson School, 14
  business trip to Texarkana, 127–128
  and direct experience of dysfunctional judge, 102
  establishing research program, 14
  and media attention, 160
  meeting with J.F. Kennedy, 1
  meetings with Leopold Kohr, 13
  ratification of laws or constitutional addendum, 70
  reorganizing the financial service industry in Liechtenstein, 142
  speech to UN General Assembly, 14
  study of economy, 7, 72
  veto right, 71
  work for Claiborne Pell, 95
health care, 111–112
health insurance, 111–112
Hitler, Adolf, 38–39
Holy Roman Empire (of German Nations)
  and elected emperor, 18, 26–27
  emergence of, 55
  longevity of centralized government of, 61
homo erectus, 45–48, 179–180

horses
- influence on size of states, 35
- military use of, 33, 34, 37–38, 41, 44, 53–54
- used for transportation, 32, 33

House of Commons (GB), 56, 60
House of Lords (GB), 56, 60
House of Representatives (USA), 60
human evolution
- and genetic differences, 177
- of *homo erectus*, 47–48
- influence of individuality on, 23–24
- influence of religion on, 21–22
- time span of, 48

human rights
- of a civilian population, 40–41
- efficiency of the European Court of Justice and, 103
- violations of, 161–162, 164, 174

hunter-gatherers, 17–18, 24, 30, 45, 92, 107
hunting, 46, 49
Hussein, Saddam, 43, 161

I

Iceland, 67
ideology, 22, 23, 30
- *see also* communism; liberalism; nationalism; socialism

illegal drugs, 98–100
illiteracy, 62, 65
Imperial House of Japan, 24
Inaugural Address 1961 (J.F. Kennedy), 1
India, 41, 114
Indian civilizations (Americas), 24, 30, 32
indirect democracies
- adaptation to tms model, 157–159
- and interaction with citizens, 81–82
- and the practice of buying votes in, 83
- of the USA, 59–62, 67–68
- as a weak form of democracy, 77

individuality, 23–24
Industrial Revolution, 12, 85
industrialization
- influence on size of states, 36–37, 41, 107–108

- in Liechtenstein, 11, 13
- political consequences of, 85
- spread of, 12–13

inflation, 135–136
infrastructure
- influence on size of states, 31–33, 34
- repair after military intervention, 169–170
- state interference in, 121

instincts, 21
insurance industry, 111–112, 144
intelligence, 23–24
international crime, 91, 98
Iraq, 43, 164, 168–174
Iraq War, 43
Islam, 27, 34–35, 36
Islamic empires, 27, 34
Israel, 86, 148, 164

J

Japan
- divine status of emperor of, 24, 53
- expansion of, 37
- industrialization of, 36–37
- transformation into democratic state, 162
- and US military supremacy, 41–42

Jesus of Nazareth, 26
Jews, 34
job security, 79
Judaism, 24, 25
judges
- appointed by the US president, 60
- dismissal of, 102, 105–106
- duties and responsibilities in the tms constitution, 153, 197–199
- election of, 60, 73, 102
- independence of, 101
- proposed by parliament Liechtenstein, 73
- shortage of, 103

judicial system
- adaptation after military intervention, 166–167
- independence of, 101
- of Liechtenstein, 73
- organization in the tms constitution of, 153, 197–199

of the Roman Empire, 33
in the USA, 60
Jura (canton), 7
justice, 22

K
Kennedy, John F., 1
KGB (secret police), 8
Kohr, Leopold (1909-94), 12
Korean War, 39–40
Kurds, 169, 171, 174
Kuwait, 148

L
labor force
  in ancient agrarian states, 50–51
  lack of, 13, 14
  use of foreign labor, 11, 14
labor market, reforms, 112–113
Latin America, 162
law
  adaptation after military intervention, 166
  adaptation to tms model, 161
  and the banking system, 142–143
  citizens and the, 91, 94, 97–98
  enforcement of, 91–92, 97
  implementing international, 94
  influence of Roman, 52
  legitimized by religion, 21, 24
  production of, 93–94
  reform of production of, 95–96
  during Roman Empire, 33, 52
liberalism, 79–80
liberalization, 14
Liechtenstein Global Trust, 142
Liechtenstein Institute on Self-Determination (Princeton University), 14–15, 161
Liechtenstein law gazette, 72
Liechtenstein National Bank, 138–141
Liechtenstein (Principality)
  see also Liechtenstein's constitution;
    Princely House of Liechtenstein
  the currency of, 137–141
  deposing of head of state of, 72
  and economic ties with Austria, 11, 69
  and economic ties with Switzerland, 11, 69, 137–138
  economy of, 10–13
  educational system, 117
  financial services industry in, 142
  fundamental rights of direct democracy in, 66–67
  influence legal development Austria on, 69, 101
  judicial system, 73
  media in, 160
  member of the UN, 14
  membership of EEA, 167, 174
  as monarchy with democratic legitimation, 57, 71–73
  position of monarchy in, 15–16, 71–74, 75
  public finances of, 130
  and the referendum, 70
  and the right of initiative, 70, 74
  and the right of self-determination, 15, 74–75, 88–89
  size of parliament in, 96–97
  support for the unemployed in, 112
  and tax competition, 130–131
Liechtenstein thaler, 138–141
Liechtensteinische Landesbank (LLB), 142
Liechtensteinische Gesetzessammlung, 72
Liechtenstein's constitution
  of 1862, 69
  of 1921, 69–70, 73, 101
  as base for the tms constitution, 151–155
  based on direct democracy, 56, 69, 70
  and the development of democracy, 68
  revision of 2003, 72–73, 101
liquidity, 143–145
loans, 129
local communities
  see also political units
  and authority for direct taxation, 127, 128–129, 130
  bankruptcies of, 129–130
  laws and regulations of, 100
  organization and duties in the tms constitution, 153, 200
  and ownership of mineral rights, 132–133

and proportional representation in tms
    constitution, 153, 190–194
and the right of self-determination, 74
and tax competition, 130–131
voucher system for the educational
    system, 117
in the welfare system, 113
Louis XIV, King of France, 29

M

machine guns, 38
market economy
    and agriculture, 123–124
    and the drug problem, 99–100
    and property rights, 92–93
    and the Soviet Union, 41
    and the Turkish Empire, 36
Masada, 33
mass-production, 12, 13, 36, 41
materialistic society, 23, 110
media, 147, 159–160
merchants, 54–55
metal currencies, 135–136, 137–141
Middle Ages
    military technology in, 31
    role of religion in, 21, 26, 27–28
    size of states in, 10, 12
    unity in Europe during, 27
    use of cavalries in, 33, 34
military intervention, 43, 148, 161–162, 164–172
military superpowers, 41–43
military technology, 31–36, 38–44, 164
mineral rights, 131–133
minimum wages, 110–111
minister of defense, 153
ministers, 104, 153, 195–196
ministry of foreign relations, 104
ministry of justice, 104
ministry of the interior, 153
minorities, 87–88
    see also ethnic minorities; religious minorities
Monaco, 16
monarchies

definition of, 18
with democratic legitimation, 55
duties and responsibilities in tms
    constitution, 183–184
hereditary, 51
hereditary, combined state model with
    oligarchy, 30, 49–51, 53–54
hereditary, with democratic legitimation,
    57, 71–73
hereditary, with religious legitimation, 5,
    33, 49–50, 53
necessity of oligarchy in, 81–82, 84
part in state cycle, 19, 45, 47
reduced power of, 56
with religious legitimation, 50, 55
role of, in Liechtenstein, 15–16, 71–72, 75
symbolic value of, 56
taxation policy of, 54–55
monarchs
    deposing of, 72
    divine status of, 24, 49, 51
    loss of privacy and freedom of speech,
        56–57
    position in tms constitution, 152, 185–187
    versus presidents, 97
    representational role of, 56–57, 71
    role of, in Liechtenstein, 71–74, 97
    and veto right in tms constitution, 153, 201
monasteries, 27–28
Mongols, 34
Montesquieu, Charles de Secondat, 19
Moravia (Czech Republic), 6
multi-ethnic states, 6, 8
Myanmar (formerly Burma), 149

N

Napoleon I, Emperor of France, 63
Napoleonic Empire, 63
Napoleonic wars, 37
NASA (National Aeronautics and Space
    Administration), 180
national currency, 135–145
National Socialism, 2–3
nationalism
    destructive influence of, 5–6

and globalization, 78–79, 81
ideology of, 63–65
replacing liberalism, 80
as state legitimation, 5, 30
triggered by economic crisis of 1929, 162
Native American cultures, 32
Native Americans, 24, 30, 32
NATO (North Atlantic Treaty Organization), 43, 148–149
Nazi Germany
see The Third Reich
Neanderthal man, 46
Near East, 32, 49
The Needham Question, 36
NGOs (non-governmental organizations), 149
nomadic tribes, 53, 54
non-governmental organizations (NGOs), 149
North American Free Trade Agreement, 174
North Atlantic Treaty Organization, 43, 148–149
North Korea, 39–40, 86, 87, 149
NPT (Nuclear Non-Proliferation Treaty), 86
Nuclear Non-Proliferation Treaty (NPT), 86
nuclear weapons, 86, 148

O

OECD (Organization for Economic Cooperation and Development), 122, 123, 147
oil, 7
oligarchies
based on democratic legitimation, 55–56, 67–68, 69, 82–84
characteristics of pure, 82
definition of, 18
membership of, 54–55
and monarchies, 30, 49–51, 53–54
necessity of, 81–82
part in state cycle, 19, 45, 47
and resistance to giving up power, 77–78
taxation policy, 54–55
and the welfare state, 109
Organisation of African Unity, 148–149
Organization for Economic Cooperation and Development (OECD), 122, 123, 147
Organization for Security and Cooperation in Europe (OSCE), 103
Organization of American States, 148–149
Orthodox Church, 26
OSCE (Organization for Security and Cooperation in Europe), 103

P

"Panzerfaust," 39
papacy, 26–27
paper currencies, 136, 138
parliaments
and governments, 105
power of, 56
size of, 96–97
in tms constitution, 152–153, 190–194
peasant revolts, 55
Pell, Claiborne, 95
pensions, 109–111, 129
Perry, Matthew Calbraith, 37
philately, 10
police force
on community level, 100
and law enforcement, 97–98
as task force after military intervention, 165–166, 168, 169, 171
in the tms constitution, 153
political parties, 62, 101–102, 105, 108, 158–159
"political recipes," 1
political units
see also local communities
autonomy of, 60–61, 67
in France, 64
in Liechtenstein, 88–89
and political power, 77–78
and right of self-determination, 74, 88
politicians
adaptation to tms model, 157–159
and the practice of buying votes, 83, 95–96
and the welfare state, 109
popular vote
see also referendum

consultative character of, 69
in direct democracies, 98
in Liechtenstein, 71–74, 97
right of, 66–67
in Switzerland, 105
in the tms constitution, 187, 191, 192–193, 197, 201
in the USA, 60, 105
population density, 24
Portugal, 35
post-colonial states, 6
postage stamps, 10
postal services, 147
presidents
 appointing judges (US), 60
 independence of, 89
 as monarchs, 18, 67, 97
 position in tms constitution, 152, 185–187
 veto right of, 97
prime ministers, 53, 104, 195
Princely House of Liechtenstein
 see also Hans-Adam II, Prince of Liechtenstein
 criticism of, 71, 72–73
 deposing of Prince of, 72
 finances of, 3, 71–72
 house law of, 72, 74, 75
 manner of succession, 72
 support for self-determination, 15–16, 74
 ties with the House of Habsburg, 6–7, 69
Princeton University (New Jersey), 14–15, 161
privatization
 of educational system, 117
 of mineral rights, 132–133
 of postal services, 147
 of railroad system, 124
 of road system, 124
 of state enterprises after dictatorship, 170
prohibition, 99
property rights, 92–93
protectionism, 13, 80, 114–115
Protestant Church, 28, 29
Protestant Reformation, 28, 65

Prussian-Austrian War (1866), 37
public finances, 127–133
public liability, 153, 200
Punic Wars, 52

Q
Québec, 9

R
radio, 147, 160
railroads, 13, 32, 121–122, 124
referendum, 66–67, 70, 73, 97, 184, 193
 see also popular vote
Reformation, 28, 65
refugee problem, 162–163, 170, 171
reincarnation, 22
religion
 see also Buddhism; Christianity; Islam; Judaism
 freedom of, 61
 and the French Revolution, 63
 influence on history, 26–28, 29, 65
 influence on social behavior, 22–23
 persecution of, 22, 29, 59
 role of, in the Middle Ages, 21, 26, 27–28
 separation from state, 61
 as state legitimation, 3, 19, 21, 24–27
 as state legitimation, during agrarian revolution, 49–50, 51
 as state legitimation, for monarchies, 5, 55
 as state legitimation, in Roman Empire, 33
 as state legitimation, worldwide, 30
religious minorities, 24–25, 34, 59
religious tolerance, 25–26, 28–29, 34
retirement age, 110
revolutions, 55
right of initiative, 67, 70
rivers, 32
roads, 13, 32, 122, 124
rocket launcher, 39
Roman Catholic Church
 see also Reformation
 influence on economy, 27–28, 29
 influence on European history, 26–28, 29
 and liberalism, 80

in Switzerland, 65
Roman Empire
   see also Roman Republic
   as example of large state, 10
   and hereditary monarchy, 33
   infrastructure in, 32–33
   judicial and legislative systems, 33
   and mass-production, 36
   religion as state legitimation, 33
   religious tolerance in, 25–26
   spread of Christianity in, 25–26
   taxation policy of, 55
Roman Kingdom, 52
Roman Republic
   see also Roman Empire
   central role of religion in state authority of, 21
   civil wars in, 50
   emergence of, 51
   law and political structure in, 52
   and the practice of buying votes in, 83
Russia
   see Soviet Union
Russian Revolution, 30
Russo-Japanese War (1905), 36–37

S

school attendance, compulsory, 117, 118, 184
Second World War, 38–39
self-determination
   in Algerian context, 5
   in Basque context, 5
   in Canadian context, 9
   and ethnicity, 74–75
   in the EU states, 154–155
   in Liechtenstein's context, 15, 74–75, 88–89
   as a means to avoid conflict/bloodshed, 9–10, 14
   in practice, 15–16
   in Russian context, 8
   and size of political units, 88
   in Swiss context, 7
   UN Charter on, 15
   in Yugoslavian context, 9–10

Senate (USA), 60
Serbia, 9
serfdom, 54
   see also slavery
settlement patterns, 47, 122, 124–125
shipping, 35
Singapore, 6
Sino-Japanese Wars, 37
Six-Day War (1967), 148
slavery, 62, 63
"small is beautiful" humanitarian theory, 12
social behavior
   connection with politics, 25
   guided by instincts, 21, 107–108, 178
   guided by intelligence, 23–24
   of *homo erectus*, 45–48
social control, 107–108
socialism
   in combination with nationalism, 63–65
   compared to National Socialism, 2–3
   destructive force of, 6
   and globalization, 78–79, 81
   replacing liberalism with, 80
   as state legitimation, 5, 30
society, materialistic, 23, 110
solvency, 143–145
South Korea, 6, 39–40
sovereignty
   see self-determination
Soviet Empire, 7–8
   see also Soviet Union
Soviet Union
   collapse of, 8, 14, 22
   expansion of, 37
   in the Korean War, 39–40
   and the market economy, 41
   political murders in, 2–3
   reforms under Gorbachev, 174
   secession of republics of, 74
space travel, 180–181
Spain, 35
stamps, 10
state pensions, 109–111
states
   see also democracies; monarchies; oligarchies

based on democratic legitimation, 30, 55
based on dynastic legitimation, 28, 29–30
based on ideological legitimation, 30
based on religious legitimation, 3, 19, 24–27, 29–30, 49–50, 51, 77
centralized versus decentralized, 65
on collapse and reform of, 7–8
cycle of types of, 19, 45, 47
definition of, 17
development of, 48–50, 53, 59, 107
financing, 51
future designs for, 85, 86–89
Greek classification of types of, 18, 45
and interaction with citizens, 81–82
international organization of, 86
life cycles of, 179–180
and the maintenance of law, 91–92
and mineral rights, 132–133
origins of, 17–19
separation from religion, 61
as service company, 3, 4, 80, 81, 87, 94, 97, 100, 130, 178
size of, 10–13, 31–44, 53
structure of, 59–61, 65–67
territorial changes of, 179
Stone Age
 elements of democracy in communities in the, 45–46
 hierarchical structures of tribes in the, 18, 46–48
 property rights in the, 92
 settlement patterns in the, 47
 size of states in the, 24, 31–32
storage economies, 49, 50
subsidies, 154
Suez crisis (1956), 164
suffrage, 62, 63
Sumerians, 17
Sunni Triangle, 171–172
Supreme Court (US), 60
Sweden, 35
Swiss constitution, 65
Swiss franc, 139
Switzerland
 canton autonomy, 61, 67, 104

constitution based on direct democracy, 56
diversity of population, 65
economic ties with Liechtenstein, 11, 69, 137–138
fundamental rights of direct democracy in, 66–67
lack of labor force in, 14
media in, 160
model of government, 104
and the referendum, 66–67, 70
and the right of initiative, 67, 70
and the right of self-determination, 7
state structure of, 65–67
and tax competition, 130–131
and women's suffrage, 63

T
taxation policy
 in ancient agrarian states, 51
 caused by WW I, 136
 changed by parliament, 56
 in Liechtenstein, 10–11
 local communities and, 119
 of monarchies and oligarchies, 54–55
 of the Roman Empire, 55
 and tax competition, 130–131
 of the tms model, 127–129, 130
 of the US, 127–128
television, 147, 160
terrorism, 42, 148, 166, 170, 171
terrorist organizations, 100
Texarkana (US), 127–128
"the bigger the better" economic theory, 10–13
Theodosius I, Emperor, 26
third millennium state constitution
 see also third millennium state model
 based on Liechtenstein's constitution, 151–155
 duties and responsibilities of the government in, 153, 195–196
 duties and responsibilities of the state in, 152
 organization and duties of local communities in, 153, 200

organization of parliament in, 152–153, 190–194
organization of the judicial system in, 153, 197–199
position of monarchs or presidents in, 152, 185–187
procedures for changing the, 153–154, 201
public liability in, 153, 200
rights and obligations of citizens in, 152, 188–189
as a substitute for the EU draft constitution, 154–155
third millennium state model
see also third millennium state constitution
agriculture in the, 123–124
conditions for, 85, 86–89
from democratic constitutional states to, 157–161
from dictatorship to, 161–174
educational system of, 117–119
health insurance in, 111–112
integrating people into the direct democracy of, 97
justice system in, 101
laws and regulations of, 93–96
no financing through debts, 129
and ownership of mineral rights, 132–133
pensions in, 110–111, 129
retreating from the welfare system, 113
settlement patterns in, 124–125
size of government, 104
size of parliament in, 96–97
support for the unemployed in, 112–113
taxation policy of, 127–129, 130
transportation in the, 123–124
welfare system in, 113
The Third Reich, 2–3, 11, 87, 161
Third World countries
see developing countries
Thirty Year's War, 28
"Thousand Year Reich," 39
Tokugawas, 53, 56
totalitarian state, 2
tourism, 10

trade
and globalization, 79
impact of waterways on, 12
liberalization of European, 11
liberalization of world, 14
in Stone Age tribal communities, 47
transportation
high efficiency of, 86
influence on settlement patterns, 122
railroad networks used for, 13
road networks used for, 13, 32
state intervention in, 121–122
in the tms model, 123–124
waterways used for, 12, 32
tribal communities, 18, 47
Turkey, 32
Turkish Empire, 35, 36, 38

U
UN General Assembly, 14
UN (United Nations)
and the Council of Europe, 103
and democracy after military intervention, 163
and international law, 94
and the Korean War, 39–40
Liechtenstein's entry into the, 14
military intervention by the, 148
role in foreign policy, 148–149
and self-determination, 15
unemployment, 112–113, 114–115
United Nations (UN)
see UN (United Nations)
United States Congress, 60
United States of America (USA)
see also American Constitution; American Revolution; Civil War (USA)
control of indirect taxation in the, 127–128
diversity of population in the, 65
and entering WW I, 38
and establishing democracy after military intervention, 164–166, 172–173
judicial system in, 60
in the Korean War, 39–40

and military interventions, 43, 162, 164
and military supremacy, 41–43
model of government in the, 104–105
and opening up of Japan, 37
and ownership of mineral rights, 131–132
postal services in the, 147
and the practice of buying votes in the, 83
religiosity of the, 61
replacement of civil servants in the, 106
state autonomy of the, 60–61, 67
state structure of the, 59–60, 61, 67
and suffrage, 62
and trade with Europe, 11
in the Vietnam wars, 40
University of St. Gallen, 7
US dollar, 138, 139, 165
US Federal Reserve Board, 138
USSR
  see Soviet Union

V

Verwaltungs- und Privatbank (VPB), 142
veto right, 71, 97, 153, 201
Vienna, 35
Vietnam wars, 40
Von Bismarck, Otto, 109
voters
  and credibility of party programs, 62
  in a direct democracy, 98
  expectations of, 78
  and the practice of buying votes, 83, 95–96
voucher system, educational, 117–119, 130, 150, 184

W

wars
  see also under names of specific wars
  the danger from, 147–148
  influence on population, 55
  prevention of, 86
  undesirability of, 178
waterways, 12, 32, 34
weapons
  see under specific weapons

weapons industry, 41–42
weapons of mass destruction, 86, 148
welfare state, 78, 108–113
Western Europe
  and the arms race in artillery, 35
  change of power structures in, 28
  influence of religion on history of, 26–28, 29
  politically diversity of, 26–27
  religious tolerance in, 28
  unification of, 42–43, 64
white-collar criminality, 91, 98
Wilson, Woodrow, 14
Winkler, Günther, 103
Woodrow Wilson School of Public and International Affairs (Princeton University), 14
work force
  see labor force
World Health Organization, 148–149
World Trade Organization (WTO), 127, 148–149
World War I, 37–38, 136
World War II, 38–39
WTO (World Trade Organization), 127, 148–149

Y

Yugoslavia, 9–10, 14, 161

Z

Zwingli, Huldrych, 65